Garden Ornament

George Plumptre

With special contributions by Jamie Garnock and James Rylands

Photographs by Hugh Palmer

With 506 illustrations, 150 in colour

Garden Ornament

FIVE HUNDRED YEARS OF HISTORY AND PRACTICE

 THAMES AND HUDSON

The photographs in this book are dedicated to my mother, Stella Palmer

On the half-title page: 'The Water Parterre', engraving by Isaac de Caus, c. 1645.
On the title-page: 'Roma Antica', a model formerly in the garden of the Villa d'Este, Tivoli, from G. de Rossi, *Le Fontane di Roma*, Rome, 1675.
On the Contents page: antique urn from G. B. Piranesi, *Vasi, Candelabri, Cippi, Sarcofagi* . . ., 1778.

© 1989 Thames and Hudson
Texts © 1989 George Plumptre, Jamie Garnock, James Rylands
Photographs © 1989 Hugh Palmer

Filmset in Great Britain by FMT Graphics Ltd
Printed and bound in Japan

CONTENTS

Preface

GARDEN ORNAMENT is a subject of great depth and variety, both historically and in terms of the different categories of ornament.

In order to achieve the desired breadth of coverage the book is divided into three main sections. In the first an historical introduction and overview of the evolution of garden ornament, concentrating upon those countries where, during different eras, the progress was particularly decisive and influential, is followed by historical discussion of the major categories of ornament as they have emerged through the centuries.

Garden Ornament's fundamental theme is the evolution and employment of ornament in the Western garden. While the importance of the gardens of the ancient world — and of oriental cultures — is recognized, the decisive launching point of continuous development is taken as the Italian Renaissance. In the historical introduction, therefore, a preliminary section discussing the Renaissance and the subsequent shift in the mainstream of progress from Italy to France and then to England, sets the scene before the more general chronological section which follows.

In the second section, Jamie Garnock discusses the use of ornament in the contemporary garden. Here it is pointed out that while much use is made of well-established precedents, styles and examples, the contemporary garden has witnessed the evolution of new attitudes to the use of ornament, creating a flexible technique that can incorporate modern artistic styles and often display refreshing originality. Jamie Garnock offers wide-ranging advice upon a host of situations or problems which face the aspiring ornamental gardener, drawing upon his first-hand experience as a garden designer in both the United Kingdom and the United States.

Practical information is also the essence of the third section, by James Rylands, the Sotheby's expert from their Billinghurst office which concentrates upon the sale of all types of garden ornament and associated architectural artefacts. His catalogue of ornament surveys items currently available, providing factual information concerning their date and place of origin, the materials they are made of and their proportions. Each entry has its own illustration.

The three main sections of the book are followed by a Bibliography where both works referred to in the preparation of *Garden Ornament* and a selection of historically important publications are included, and by a list of suggested suppliers in the United Kingdom and the United States.

George Plumptre

HISTORICAL INTRODUCTION

George Plumptre

*God Almighty first planted a garden; and indeed
it is the purest of human pleasures. It is the greatest refreshment
of the spirit of man.*

FRANCIS BACON

One of the most perfect *of all gardens is that of Isola Bella in Lake Maggiore. The site
was chosen for his villa by Count Carlo Borromeo in the 17th century and he turned the
whole island into a garden. Its ten terraces look over the lake, the various levels emphasized
by the dramatic placing of statuary and other forms of ornament.*

The ornamental garden in the West

THE ORIGINS of the ornamental garden, as it has been understood in the West for the last four hundred years, lie in the Italian Renaissance. The Medici gardens around Florence are its prototypes, but if a specific time and place were to be chosen for its birth, it would have to be Rome in 1503, when Bramante was commissioned by Pope Julius II to design the Cortile del Belvedere in the Vatican. As Georgina Masson has put it: 'With this one plan Bramante dictated the basis of European garden design for more than two centuries to come.'

Bramante's task was to redesign the court linking the Papal Palace with the old Villa Belvedere as a grand ornamental garden. His architectural treatment of the sloping terrain, incorporating a grand central axis and perspective crossed by a series of terraces, the different levels linked by stairways, established a blueprint for all subsequent gardens of the High Renaissance. At the top was Julius's *giardino segreto* and beyond, the focal-point of a curving niche where his collection of antique statues was displayed.

The pattern devised by Bramante enabled the Italians to capitalize on the hilly surroundings in which they built their villas, transforming them into gardens of spectacular appearance. The basic plan remained the same in numerous settings: a major axis leading away from the villa, given great perspective by thickly planted trees or *bosco* on either side. The axis descends or ascends in a series of architectural levels marked by terraces held up by often massive retaining walls surmounted by balustrades, decorated with fountains, urns and statues and linked by sweeping stairways. The terraces terminate at both ends in the *bosco*, thereby maintaining the thread of humanist theory of the garden as a place for man and his natural surroundings and marking the progression from the garden into the countryside beyond.

Bramante's Cortile del Belvedere in the early 16th century. On the left is the Vatican palace, on the right the old Villa Belvedere, lying behind the giant niche. Bramante connected the two by a series of steps and terraces. The large lower court was used for pageants.

As if to celebrate this architectural release, the gardens became imbued with the artistic vigour and exuberance characteristic of the High Renaissance. This was most often achieved by the use of water and nowhere to more spectacular effect than at the Villa d'Este near Tivoli, begun shortly after 1550. The villa and garden were designed for Cardinal Ippolito d'Este by Pirro Ligorio who was assisted in his conception of the various water features by the engineer Orazio Oliveri.

The Villa d'Este, Tivoli, an engraving by Piranesi, 1773. This garden has never been surpassed for its lavish and inventive use of water, made possible by the steeply sloping site. It is now more densely wooded, but the various channels, fountains, water-steps and cascades are as spectacular as when they were built.

No doubt part of the inspiration for the Villa d'Este's almost excessively lavish and dramatic appearance derived from Ippolito's determination to outdo his rival, Cardinal Alessandro Farnese, who had commissioned Vignola to redesign the Farnese Palace at Caprarola. After Alessandro's death his grandson added the casino and its own garden, set at a distance from the great pentagon-shaped palace. Although Vignola had also died by the time the project was carried out, the design of the garden leading up to the casino was almost certainly his.

Vignola was the outstanding garden architect of the Renaissance and therefore it is entirely fitting that he should have designed the Villa Lante at Bagnaia, which is generally considered to be the most perfect expression of the Renaissance garden. The villa and garden were commissioned by Cardinal Gambera during the 1560s, to provide a suitable summer residence. In response Vignola created a garden dominated by water descending through a series of pools, fountains and cascades from terrace to terrace, between the twin pavilions of the villa to the water parterre at the bottom. If less impressive than some Renaissance gardens, it is unsurpassed in its overall harmony.

Parts of the Villa Lante give a hint of the Baroque towards which Italian gardens were moving by the end of the 16th century and which culminated in the Villa Garzoni at Collodi begun during the 1650s. The precipitous hillside site to one side of Collodi Castle was treated with incredible bravado. From a richly decorated parterre at the lowest level the garden rises through three enormous terraces linked at the centre by zig-zagging double flights of balustraded stairs. Above, the central axis is continued by a water cascade between thickly planted trees and at the top a statue of Fame blows a spout of water from her trumpet into the pool below and provides the final flourish.

In Italy the 16th and 17th centuries saw the creation of a type of garden that was to sweep Europe. The Villa Medici (above) at Castello, near Florence, comes near the beginning of that tradition. It was started in 1538 by Niccolo Tribulo, relying heavily on classical features like this stone basin which stands in a grotto and supports a group of lifesized animals. The Villa Garzoni (right), at Collodi, Tuscany, dates from the second half of the 17th century. A steeply sloping site allows an elaborate series of staircases and water cascades.

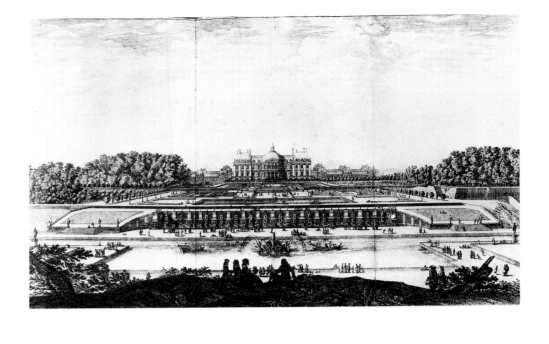

Vaux-le-Vicomte looking back towards the house. From here the canal lying at right angles to the main axis comes into its own for the first time.

The Grotto of Orpheus at St-Germain-en-Laye. The steep descent, almost a cliff, had been formed by quarrying, and was hollowed into tunnels and grottoes when the garden was laid out between 1599 and 1610.

By the middle of the 17th century the influence of the Italian Renaissance was well established throughout most of Europe, in particular in neighbouring France, where it was already in evidence in such gardens as Chantilly, Chenonceaux and the royal gardens of Fontainebleau and Saint-Germain-en-Laye. At the same time as the creation of the Villa Garzoni was marking one of the final flowerings of the Italian style, the creation of Vaux-le-Vicomte marked the achievement of a French style which, inspired by the Italian Renaissance, transcended it in grandeur and power and which was brought to a climax by Louis XIV at Versailles. If the Italian Renaissance was motivated by man's place in the universe and his relationship with nature, the great French gardens of the 17th century were inspired by the belief in man's control of nature and were illustrations of this control.

French classicism, with a strong mannerist influence, had emerged during the 16th century and steadily developed into the architectural style exemplified by the buildings and gardens of François Mansart. In garden design its principles were set out by André Mollet in his small but highly influential book, *Le Jardin de Plaisir*, published in 1651.

At Vaux-le-Vicomte Mollet's guidelines were adapted on a hitherto unprecedented scale by André le Nôtre, whose work represented the French formal style at its zenith. In 1657 Nicholas Fouquet, the Finance Minister and a man of great intelligence and taste as well as great wealth and ambition, commissioned Louis le Vau to build a château and Le Nôtre to lay out the surrounding garden, both of unrivalled splendour. Certainly Fouquet achieved his aim, but his creation, which was completed in five years, was to cause his downfall.

The genius of Le Nôtre's achievement at Vaux-le-Vicomte lay in the perfect balance and unity of the garden's component parts and features, sweeping away from the château in one huge main axis crossed at right angles by others. In the gradual progression from one level to another linked by wide flights of shallow stairs and in one place by the water cascades, through the series of parterres decorated with statues and urns, to the main cross-axis of the initially disguised canal and finally up the distant slope to the colossal statue of Hercules, nothing disturbs the sense of absolute control to which every smallest detail contributes.

Fouquet's contemporaries could not but admire his new château and garden but it aroused feelings of intense jealousy, in particular in his king, Louis XIV. Within months Louis had had Fouquet arrested and after a lengthy trial he was committed to prison where he died in 1680.

The main focus of the garden at Vaux-le-Vicomte is a giant statue of Hercules. It can be seen from the house in the far distance, but the canal that lies in between is invisible until one has actually walked half way towards it (see pp.16, 17).

Spurred on by anger at Fouquet's presumption and released by the death of Mazarin in 1661 from the limitations which the powerful minister had imposed upon his monarchy, Louis determined to build his own palace and gardens which would overshadow Vaux, but also be the visible embodiment of his power. He chose his father's hunting-lodge at Versailles which was transformed, in the series of schemes beginning in 1661 carried out by the men who had created Vaux-le-Vicomte; the architect Louis le Vau, the garden designer André le Nôtre and the painter and sculptor Charles le Brun, into the most impressive statement of absolute monarchy ever conceived.

Le Nôtre's design focused upon the huge central vista stretching away from the palace for such a distance that the limitations of space appeared to dissolve. It incorporated an awe-inspiring progression of ornamental features, each with its own designated place and significance. For Versailles as conceived by Louis XIV and executed by Le Nôtre was a grand allegory upon Louis's emblem, the Sun, and its central place in the natural world and the universe. Therefore, as André Félibien described it: 'All the figures and ornaments which one sees are not placed at random but in their order of relationship with the Sun and its personification.'

15

France took up the Italian innovations and exploited them on a much larger scale. Le Nôtre's garden at Vaux-le-Vicomte, 1656-61, slopes gently away from the house. At the end a canal (left) crosses the axis at right angles, but is not seen until the spectator has almost reached it. A high balustrade marked by sculpture additionally conceals it from the house. The mid-18th century garden at Canon, in Normandy, is more intimate in scale; especially in the series of thirteen interconnecting small, walled fruit gardens, or 'chartreuses', six of which are linked by a central path leading through archways in the dividing walls and are a feature unique to Canon. At the end is a marble statue of Pomona.

17

The perspective of Le Nôtre's main vista was increased by the trees planted in thousands on either side; into these trees axes lead off at right-angles to end in various formal parterres, *bosquets*, buildings or fountains. The provision of sufficient quantities of water was always the major problem at Versailles. The various formal *pièces d'eau*, the largest of which was the central cruciform canal 1,800 metres by 1,500, were kept constantly supplied, but we know that there was never sufficient to feed the 1,200 or so jets which the innumerable fountains contained all at the same time. The action of the fountains was regulated to correspond to the movements of the king and his courtiers, or to the effects required for a specific event or entertainment.

Within Le Nôtre's design the allegorical details were provided by the statues, groups for fountains and urns, chosen and designed by Le Brun and made by his team of sculptors and craftsmen. Never before or since has the creation of outdoor statuary achieved such a combination of quality and numbers. An important development was made in the materials used, for as well as the numerous white marble figures additional richness was given by others cast in gilded lead or bronze.

The scale of the Versailles gardens and their overpowering geometric logic enabled Louis XIV to display himself in the role of absolute monarch, serving as a reminder to the enormous court whom he kept in virtually constant attendance there of his power and the significance of that power. Formal and ornamental gardening, thus elevated beyond the realms of artistic quality, of aesthetic appreciation and of allegorical significance to a level of international politics and quasi-mystical supremacy, could progress no further.

The gardens of Versailles in the time of Louis XIV. The grand scale still remains, but many of the features shown here have since been altered or demolished, such as the circular colonnade in the right foreground.

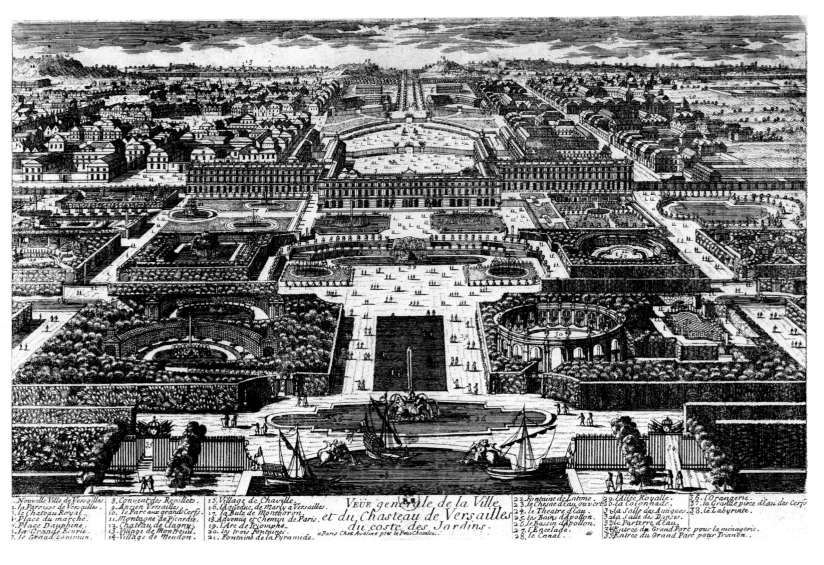

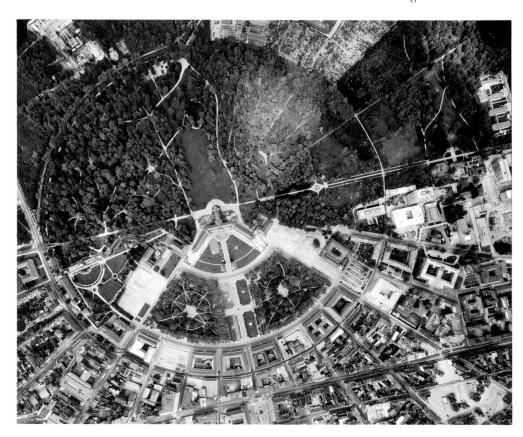

Karlsruhe, southern Germany. Several of the radiating avenues were later replaced by more picturesque, English-style planting, but the layout of the town facing it survives.

Throughout Europe the style of Versailles was emulated by many kings and princes who aspired to Louis XIV's position. Perhaps the most ambitious of these imitations was at Karlsruhe, where the Margrave's palace stands in the centre of a radiating pattern of avenues, some of which become the streets of the city while the rest form part of his enormous garden. Other German rulers were nearly as extravagant. The gardens of Pommersfelden, in Bavaria, are on almost as grand a scale, while at Sans Souci in Potsdam Frederick the Great of Prussia combined terracing, statuary, grottoes and fountains with a masterly blend of imagination and precision. But elsewhere, particularly in England, reaction was setting in. By the turn of the 18th century formality expressing man's control over nature was beginning to be rejected in favour of a more informal approach which combined appreciation of unspoiled nature with a revival of classical, Palladian architecture to produce the idealized scenes of the English landscape.

Pommersfelden, Germany, in 1728. The gardens were laid out by Lothar Franz von Schönborn, bishop of Bamberg.

Palladian England, *deprived of real classical remains, did not hesitate to build its own. West Wycombe, in Buckinghamshire, is the creation of the dilettante (and dissolute) Sir Francis Dashwood, beginning in 1750. The elliptical Temple of Venus (above), together with the flint-built 'Venus's Parlour' had both disappeared and have been reconstructed by Quinlan Terry. At Stowe, also in Buckinghamshire, the allusions are more learned. Here (right) we are looking through the Doric Arch, 1768, to the classical bridge built in 1745 and inspired by a design by Palladio.*

Claude's painting of 'Aeneas arriving at Delos' is typical of the landscape with classical ruins which English landowners of the 18th century sought to evoke in their own estates.

The mausoleum at Castle Howard, Yorkshire, designed by Nicholas Hawksmoor. Severely classical in itself, it plays a more picturesque role in the total scheme.

England had never fully accepted the uncompromising and grand formality of the French style, perhaps because of an instinctive love of countryside among Englishmen which promoted a desire to live in harmony with their surroundings rather than to mould them to their will. By the end of the seventeenth century France's influence was one of a number revealed in English gardens, along with the Dutch style introduced by William and Mary, that of the Italian Renaissance, which had come earlier in the century but whose proper progress had been interrupted by the Civil War, and the earlier style of English Tudor and Stuart gardens. Examples of this composite style are still to be seen not only in England and the Low Countries but also in Germany. The garden of the Electors of Hanover at Herrenhausen was begun in 1666. Its regular layout is divided by canals and hedges and incorporates a wealth of sculpture and ornamental urns. The courts of Hesse and Munich, among many others, could boast gardens of similar ingenuity.

During the first half of the 18th century the progress away from formalism came through the use of the natural landscape as a setting for classical buildings, inspired in part by the paintings of Claude, which depicted a tranquil unity of classicism and nature. Not surprisingly, one of the most theatrical of English architects, Sir John Vanbrugh, was in the vanguard of progress. At Castle Howard, in the 1720s, he sited his own Temple of the Four Winds at the end of a long grass terrace, and Nicholas Hawksmoor's mausoleum as a dramatic eye-catcher on a distant hill.

The man who is generally credited with having the greatest influence upon the early development of the English landscape was William Kent, who revealed unusual artistic versatility in his work as an architect, decorator, furniture-designer and gardener. Time spent in Italy prompted Kent's reverence for classical architecture and he became a protégé of Lord Burlington, the most influential patron of the early 18th century, and the foremost advocate of Palladian architecture. Kent's most significant work as a garden designer came towards the end of his career and was carried out at two places, Stowe in Buckinghamshire and Rousham in Oxfordshire, both of which survive.

Stowe was the most influential garden in England during the 18th century, not least because it evolved in stages which corresponded to the development of the landscape movement. Among all the distinguished artists and architects who worked there, Kent was perhaps the most decisive. It was his suggestions which led to the introduction of informality into an essentially formal landscape as laid out by Charles Bridgeman. The inspiration for Kent's work at Stowe is made clear in the name given to the small wooded valley, the Elysian Fields, where his work was concentrated. Overlooking the valley he built the Temple of Ancient Virtue, based on the Temple of the Sybil at Tivoli and, facing it from a distance, the Temple of British Worthies containing busts of leading Englishmen by the two outstanding sculptors of the time, Michael Rysbrack and Peter Scheemakers.

Kent's most delightful creation was the far smaller, more intimate Rousham garden, where his work survives virtually unaltered. On a wooded slope overlooking the valley of the River Cherwell, where the main river makes a large bend and a smaller stream runs down to join it, he created a wooded vale with ponds and rustic cascades called the Venus Vale and added winding walks through the wood with one path following the serpentine stream to a classical temple. Other buildings were added at strategic points, the most important of which was the seven-arched Praeneste, and seats looked out from the garden across the Cherwell valley to the eye-catcher of a Gothick mill. A number of the statues, such as Venus and Pan, were made in lead by Jan van Nost.

During the next half-century England was to evolve and perfect the landscape style which was not only universally adopted at home but which had a profound influence in Europe and America. Its success accounts for the disappearance of virtually all English gardens from before 1700. When taken to its majestic extreme, in the work of Lancelot 'Capability' Brown, ornament was almost completely banished and the desired effect was achieved through the creation of a harmonious picture of trees, sweeps of parkland, and water in serpentine-shaped lakes. Cattle and deer grazed almost to the front doors of the new Palladian country seats, kept out only by a sunken ha-ha. The hand of man was restricted to the distant glimpse of a balustraded bridge or the columns of a temple shrouded by trees. A new era in the history of gardens had begun.

Stowe, Buckinghamshire, was originally laid out by Bridgeman with formal avenues converging on Vanbrugh's Rotonda. The formality was later replaced by the more 'natural' landscaping of Kent and subsequently Capability Brown.

Gardens and history: from ancient Egypt to modern America

Gardens have evolved from two essential elements, plants and ornament. Of the two the plants have a longer history, from prehistoric times when gardens first emerged as domesticated agriculture. They have also been more constant because man has always needed to grow food and the cultivation of plants represents man's relationship with nature at its most fundamental and continuous.

Given the right circumstances, when he has not been preoccupied with the struggle for existence, man has been a creature of aspiration and herein lies the impetus for garden ornament. Ornament has elevated the garden from being a place of production to being a place of pleasure. In architectural forms it has enabled man to regulate the landscape. It has also enabled him to define and demonstrate his own relationship with nature and the landscape, be it one of subdued harmony or of desired supremacy. At certain historic peaks the ornamentation of gardens has produced great works of art, as well as bold and exciting illustrations of a society's sentiments towards the natural world.

Unlike horticulture, which has developed steadily around available plants and improvements in their cultivation, and which has usually been practised on both the humblest and the grandest scale, ornamental gardening has had certain important prerequisites. Because it has been expensive compared merely to growing things, it has been, until modern times, a pastime of the wealthy and privileged. Stimulated by a desire for relaxation, artistic expression and the enrichment of both mind and eye, it has been most successful in conditions of social stability, economic prosperity and intellectual and artistic activity and originality.

The evolution of garden ornament has gone through periods of both innovation and imitation, with successive civilizations drawing upon the traditions of their predecessors and integrating them into their own culture. This process reached a zenith during the Renaissance in Italy, the major watershed in the development of garden ornament. During the Renaissance the classical traditions of ancient Greece and Rome were reinterpreted and established as the backbone of garden ornament and architecture which, in the Western garden with which we are primarily concerned, they have remained ever since – at least until this century and the development of modern art.

While the gardens of China and Japan have histories as long as those of the Near East and Western worlds, and have during certain periods had an important influence upon garden ornament in some European countries, their evolution has been closely allied to the developing cultures of the two countries and therefore somewhat detached and independent rather than part of the historical mainstream.

The origins of this mainstream are to be found in the civilizations of Ancient Egypt and, to a lesser extent, Mesopotamia. We are fortunate that thanks to the wealth of material in hieroglyphics which adorn the walls of pyramids and other Egyptian remains, there is considerable evidence about and illustration of Egyptian gardens – very little of which exists in the case of Mesopotamia.

The whole culture of ancient Egypt revolved around the River Nile and the country's economy depended upon the agriculture which it supported. Given a social hierarchy which enjoyed stability for many centuries, the development of an ornamental style of gardening was a logical consequence. The gardens were created around the temples, royal palaces and the homes of important Egyptians such as high priests and they were tended by the slaves who were the country's workforce.

The terrace at Longwood, Pennsylvania, overlooks the Italian Water Garden and is therefore made into a feature for viewing. Beneath it a series of urns, fountains and trellises give character to the retaining wall.

The most important general feature of Egyptian gardens was that they were designed in a formal, orderly style, a precedent which has been followed ever since. At an early stage the gardens were enclosed, originally for seclusion and privacy. Later the brick walls provided the opportunity for ornamentation in the form of patterned brickwork and tiled coping along their tops, and with gates and doorways. Because of the country's heat and the arid surroundings to the Nile valley, trees and water were highly prized. Trees were planted in geometric rows while water was contained in rectangular pools and canals. Other important features were wooden pergolas to support vines, many of them with carved and painted pillars; terraces joined by stairways as a means of linking a garden of different levels; and the decoration of gardens with statues of kings, deities and sphinxes, and with large earthenware pots containing small trees and shrubs.

There is no doubt that the Egyptians were influenced in their gardening by what had been established in the older civilizations of Mesopotamia, but evidence of the extent and general appearance of Mesopotamian gardens is scarce. We do know, however, that ornamental gardens were created in the cradle of Western civilization between the Tigris and Euphrates rivers, some on the terraces of the great ziggurats, others around palaces and temples. Water, contained in formal pools and canals, was essential, as it was in Egypt and has been in the gardens of most countries — especially those with a hot climate — ever since. Again the overall plan was regular and geometric, thereby providing a satisfying sense of order.

The importance of water in ancient Egyptian gardens is charmingly illustrated in this mural from a tomb at Thebes. The owner is shown raising water for his garden by means of a pole with a bucket on one end and a weight on the other. These devices are still used today.

In Islamic gardens water is used in ways that have few parallels in the West. Here, at Shalamar Bagh, in Lahore (right), a place for sitting in the midst of the pool is reached by flat causeways at water level. In Granada, Spain (below), one can still recapture the cool tranquillity of the Moorish courtyard garden.

.Both Mesopotamia and Egypt were conquered by the ancient Persians, features of whose gardens show clear descent from the two countries. Despite being fierce conquerers the Persians made considerable developments in ornamental gardening and were to establish the tradition of what became the Islamic garden. It was with them that the concept of the garden as Paradise first emerged, as early as the time of Cyrus the Great, who established the Persian empire, and whose gardens, described by Xenophon, were called Paradise.

After the foundation of Islam during the 7th century, the tradition of the Persians provided the basis for Islamic gardens in which ornamental gardening reached new heights. Two outstanding surviving groups are the Mughal gardens of India and the Moorish gardens of Spain. Like those of their ancient forebears, Islamic gardens were formal, most often rectangular in shape and divided into quarters by four channels of water representing the four rivers of life, which flowed from a central tank or – as in many Mughal gardens – from a central pavilion. Water was an all-important element in Islamic gardens and was used with wonderful ingenuity, whether in the fountains which play in the courts of the Alhambra Palace in Spain or in the cascades or *chadars* down which great sheets of water fall from one terrrace to another in the Mughal gardens in Kashmir.

As well as their water features, Islamic gardens contained exquisite architecture, ranging from delicate pavilions providing shade to breathtaking buildings such as the Taj Mahal, or the colonnades and cloisters, with their richly carved arches and pillars, which enclosed courtyard gardens. The overall effect which was striven for was the creation of a scene of ordered beauty and repose, aspiring to the gardens of Paradise as described in the Koran.

There is virtually no surviving evidence of gardens created by the ancient Greeks. They were almost all dedicated to their gods and subservient to the temples and grottoes which they surrounded. But if they made little direct contribution to the development of ornamental gardening, the Greeks' influence upon subsequent ornamental gardening has been of fundamental importance in that the classical architecture of their temples, the statues of their gods and heroes and the style of other smaller features such as urns and vases, have dominated the ornamentation of Western gardens ever since.

Roman gardens varied from the domestic to the palatial. The urban houses of towns like Pompeii presented blank walls to the street, but inside were closed gardens where planting was cunningly used in conjunction with fountains, furniture and statues.

The importance of this influence was first evident in the gardens of ancient Rome, in particular in the villa gardens of wealthy Romans as described in great detail by Pliny the Younger. Roman gardens combined horticulture and ornament in a manner which had never been seen before and which raised the gardening art to a new level of sophistication. Garden and villa were intrinsically linked and the garden itself presented a picture of orderly balance made up of architectural features such as colonnaded porticoes copied from Greek originals, water, statues and a wide range of ornamental plants collected from all parts of the empire.

The most famous Roman villa garden was made by the emperor Hadrian near Tivoli. The enormous villa complex – more like a small town than a single residence – was built between 118 and 138 AD and the various groups of buildings and different areas were named after places which Hadrian had particularly enjoyed visiting during his travels through the Roman empire. Foremost among the garden features was the Canopus, named after the canal in the Nile delta near Alexandria, enough of which survives in original or restored form to reveal its masterly quality.

The Canopus was made in a natural valley which was enlarged to allow the canal which dominates the picture to be of sufficiently impressive proportions. The canal was surrounded by an arched colonnade with statues between the arches and, along one side, by a loggia supported by caryatids copied from the Erechtheum at Athens. At the far end of the canal was the focal-point of the whole design, the *triclinium* (or *nymphaeum*), a dining-room with an arched ceiling in the shape of an apse with water running down the curving stone of the semi-circular walls. Here Hadrian entertained and impressed his guests.

The symmetry of Hadrian's Canopus, the perfect balance of architecture, statues and water, represented a zenith in ornamental gardening in the ancient world. Like the rest of the villa, however, it did not survive intact for long after Hadrian's death. With the collapse of the Roman empire and the beginning of the Dark Ages the destruction of all such places was widespread throughout Europe. Garden making, along with all other aspects of civilized life, retreated into small protected pockets such as Christian monasteries and ornamental gardening disappeared almost completely. When it was revived over one thousand years later, excavations revealed that part of the Canopus had survived and, as the Renaissance dawned in Italy, it was destined to become a major inspiration to the garden makers of this most exciting and creative era.

Hadrian's Villa, outside Tivoli, is almost a world of its own, at least a miniature city, with baths, a theatre, libraries and gardens. The Canopus (above) is an arcaded pool with statues, recreating a place in Egypt which had particular associations for the emperor. In the model (below), it is towards the centre right, with a curved colonnade facing the triclinium at the other end. The large space bottom right is the Poikile, an allusion to the meeting place in Athens, where Hadrian had also lived.

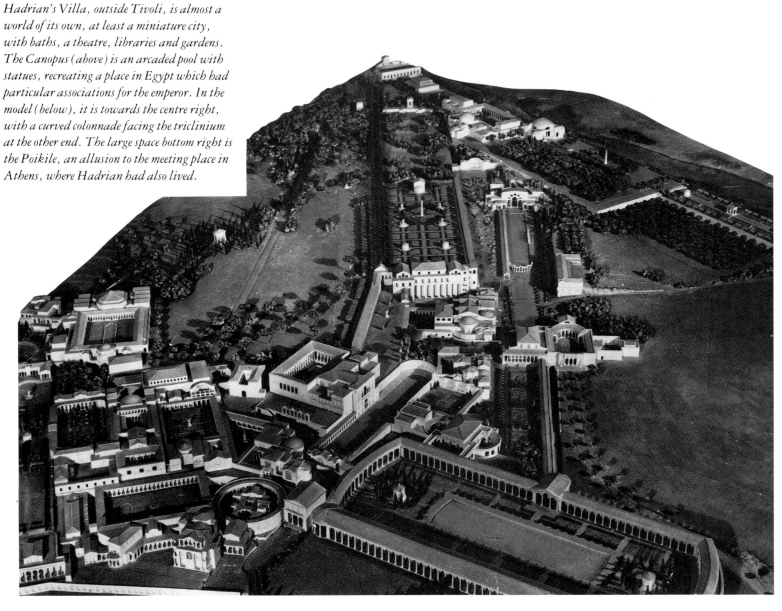

The philosophical inspiration of the Renaissance was the relationship of individual man and his surroundings, and so the creation of a garden was an ideal medium in which to examine and celebrate this relationship. The ideology behind the gardens of the Italian Renaissance was rooted in humanism, going back to the writing of Petrarch and – centuries earlier – Pliny; their style was rooted in the classicism of ancient Greece and Rome. Architectural symmetry went hand-in-hand with the aspiration to represent a state of natural order with man as the figure of central importance. It is this completeness of concept and execution which gave the gardens their astonishing strength and vitality.

In all fields of the arts the relationship between patron and artist in the Renaissance achieved a productivity which has never since been equalled, and nowhere more so than in the creation of gardens. The patrons, for whom villas with surrounding gardens became an essential part of life, as they had been for the élite of ancient Rome, were the leaders of Italy's great mercantile and financial families (notably the Medici of Florence who, by the middle of the 15th century, had acquired enormous wealth and power) and the leaders of the Church – the popes and cardinals. The men whom they commissioned were the architects, engineers and craftsmen who were the life-blood of the Renaissance and who strove towards its ideal of the *uomo universale*.

Compared with what was to follow, the early Renaissance gardens, made around the villas in the hills surrounding Florence, were subdued in both atmosphere and appearance. This was partly because they retained ties with the medieval *hortus conclusus* and also because they were primarily places for philosophical discussion, reviving the spirit of the Platonic Academy. The guidelines for the creation of these gardens were laid down by Leon Battista Alberti in his treatise *De Re Aedificatoria*, published in 1452.

The Italian humanists could be said to have rediscovered gardens, seeing them as the ideal setting for civilized amusement, conversation and music. Renaissance gardens still have something of the medieval 'hortus conclusus', a refuge from the outside world, but combined with ideas from ancient Rome. Francesco Colonna's 'Hypnerotomachia Poliphili' (1499) is an involved love-story in which gardens play a major part. Its woodcut illustrations had a lasting influence. This one shows the lovers Poliphilus and Polia at the Fountain of Venus.

*The Medici Villa Castello, outside Florence,
which Vasari called 'the most magnificent
garden in Europe'. Begun in 1538, it consisted
of a series of terraces linked on a main axis and
at each level using a statue and fountain as a
visual focus. Outside the ornamental walled
garden are areas for growing fruit and
vegetables. The grotto is shown on p.12.*

Alberti advocated a revival of the principles and design of gardens employed by
the Romans and the creation of a suitably peaceful and orderly setting for learned
conversation. Therefore, while the overall picture was classical, architecture and
ornament were only to be used when dictated by the complete design and not for
their own sake. At the Villa Careggi, Cosimo the Elder, the patriarch of the
Medici, gathered together a group who were called the Platonic Academy and his
garden closely followed the advice set down by his contemporary, Alberti.

A century later Alberti's principles of garden making were carried to probably
their highest limits at the Medici Villa at Castello. The garden was designed for
Cosimo the Great, Duke of Tuscany, by Niccolò Tribolo and while the plan is
conservative in its reserved simplicity, an important break with Alberti's limitations is marked in the fountains and statues. The original centrepiece to the main
walled garden, which rises gently away from the villa uphill to the entrance to the
grotto set in the enclosing wall, was a fountain by Tribolo surmounted by a statue
of Venus (sometimes referred to as Florence rising from the Water) by Giambologna. This was replaced in the 18th century by the present statue of Hercules and
Antaeus by Ammanati. Crouching among trees beyond the upper wall is the
colossal stone figure 'The Apennines' also by Ammanati. Set in the garden's upper
wall, on the main central axis, is the pillared entrance to the grotto.

The decisive step from the contemplative garden to the garden whose main point is visual excitement was taken, as we have seen, at Bramante's Cortile del Belvedere in 1503. The essential values of this type of layout — axial, sophisticated, artificial in every sense— remained paramount for two hundred years, dominating the whole of garden history, from the great Italian masterpieces, through the vast formal gardens of France to the England of Vanbrugh and Kent (see pp. 10-23) and indeed beyond.

The Zwinger, in Dresden, was exactly the sort of festive architecture which had its place in gardens, though in fact it was a parade ground attached to the royal palace. It consisted of a highly ornamented gate, ranges of galleries and a central pavilion acting as a grandstand.

Opposite: the octagon and cascade at Wilhelmshöhe. Planned by Giovanni Guarniero, its most spectacular feature is a great cascade incorporating statues and grottoes. The building at the top, surmounted by an obelisk carrying a copy of the Farnese Hercules, is the reservoir.

In Germany the story of gardens is similar to that of architecture. At a time when the Baroque impetus had waned in Italy, the rulers of the small German courts took it up with renewed vigour, transforming it into something lighter, less serious, more playful, and producing the late flowering that is known as Rococo. The masterpiece of this style is perhaps the Zwinger at Dresden, an ornamental courtyard that has all the characteristics of a garden except planting. Elsewhere, the same style was expanded to fill extensive parks. At Wilhelmshöhe, outside Kassel, the layout, begun in 1701, was supervised by an Italian. Its focal feature is an enormous cascade, clearly suggested by Italian models, but on an even vaster scale. Even this was only a third of what was originally planned. Veitshochheim, in Bavaria, dates from later in the century and is less spectacular than Wilhelmshöhe. But it excels in the variety and boldness of its sculpture — over three hundred figures of gods, ladies of the court, musicians and animals (including the winged horse Pegasus) as well as garden furniture of amazing, if uncomfortable, Rococo shapes.

In England, by this date, a wholly new style had emerged — introduced by William Kent and his contemporaries — which was to sweep most of Europe. At Stowe and Rousham the quality of visual surprise is still there, but the overall approach has relaxed to take account of natural features; a strong element of informality and the landscape is allowed to play its part.

Typical of this progression from the garden as expressing control over nature to the garden as harmony with nature is Stourhead, in Wiltshire. It is at once the climax of the idealized natural landscape and the moment of the discovery, attributed by Horace Walpole to Kent, that 'all Nature is a garden'.

Stourhead was created by Henry Hoare, one of the many talented amateurs who were practising as both architects and gardeners during the 18th century. Here landscape has become detached from garden, and the house, out of sight some distance away, plays no part in the design.

Around a large, irregularly shaped lake, made by damming the existing stream, surrounded by sloping woods, Hoare planned his garden as a progression from one classical building to another, each with its own significance. As well as the temples such as the Pantheon, he included a large grotto, a rustic hermitage and, at one end, a five-arched bridge and the Bristol Cross, a genuine Gothic monument relocated. Horace Walpole described Stourhead as 'one of the most picturesque places in the world'.

In the work of 'Capability' Brown classical allusion, and indeed all architectural ornament, virtually disappeared and the boundaries between garden and surrounding countryside were removed. The acceptance of open parkland as the ideal setting for a country house continued after his death in 1783. Its most successful exponent towards the end of the 18th century was Humphry Repton. Repton's work did reveal an important development, however, in that he accepted that some garden around the house, in the form of flower-beds or terraces, was a desirable prelude to the surrounding park.

To this extent, Repton hinted at the change that was to come early in the 19th century when gardens once again attained supremacy over landscape. As the writings of John Loudon show, gardening was no longer the exclusive domain of the upper classes but was hankered after by the emerging Victorian middle classes. With no one style dominant and with new plants constantly becoming available from overseas, English gardens embarked upon a period of eclecticism which continued throughout the 19th century and into the beginning of the 20th.

Gardens throughout continental Europe continued to be dominated by the ornamental formality of the Italian and French styles during the 18th century, but by its later decades the influence of the English landscape had spread and was evident in gardens such as Canon in Normandy. In one feature, the Chinese kiosk

Stourhead in Wiltshire is set in a wooded valley watered by the river Stour. Here Henry Hoare in the 1740s created an Arcadian world full of classical and poetic allusions, and artfully informal in its succession of buildings and images. The grotto (above) is a circular domed space lit from above, one part of it containing a statue of a river god. Right: the Temple of Apollo (1765) seen across the lake from the Temple of Flora (1745).

Gothic and oriental tastes in the 19th century: Repton's design for a fountain at Ashridge (above left), and the Chinese pagoda fountain of Alton Towers (above right), designed by Robert Abraham and made of cast iron.

At Trentham Park, Staffordshire, Sir Charles Barry laid out extensive gardens in the revived Italianate style that became fashionable as a reaction against the Picturesque in the 1840s. Symmetrical gravel paths, clipped hedges, steps and balustrades reappeared after an interval of a hundred years.

which stands as the focal-point at the end of a main vista, Canon also revealed the oriental influence which became popular in many gardens and which was practised in England by Sir William Chambers, who added the Chinese pagoda to the royal gardens at Kew. The Chinese style was to see its most dramatic application in England during the 19th century, at Alton Towers in Staffordshire, in parts of Biddulph Grange, also in Staffordshire and, later, at Whatton in Leicestershire.

Gardens such as these were, however, individual and unusual. In most large Victorian gardens Italianate or French formality was the rule. The aim was to be both impressive and decorative: the result was often opulent and sometimes garish. Brightly coloured flower parterres were decorated with statues, urns and seats, and formal rose gardens centred upon metalwork arbours, all of which were reproduced in large quantities by new industrial techniques, and in particular through the use of artificial stone and cast iron.

Both in England and on the Continent most 19th-century garden design and ornament was derivative. Linderhof, one of Ludwig II's Bavarian estates, combines Italianate features with English Picturesque and French formality, plus heavy overtones from Wagnerian Romanticism (one grotto contains Lohengrin's swan-drawn boat). The centrepiece is a fountain consisting of a single immensely tall water-spout that Louis XIV would certainly have envied, water-pressure being less of a problem in the Bavarian Alps than on the levels of Versailles. The garden of the Eremitage at Bayreuth is also in its way deeply Romantic, with its quiet pools, dripping grottoes and artificial ruins.

England at this time was again wide open to influences from abroad. Sir Charles Barry's terraced gardens such as Shrublands Park were inspired by the Italian Renaissance, while the complex parterres laid out by William Nesfield, another leading figure in Victorian gardening, recalled those of 17th-century France. Statues and urns were copies of famous classical figures or reproductions of well-established designs. Novelty was provided by the flood of plants, especially into England where new species were to transform the appearance of gardens.

Two German gardens. Linderhof, in Bavaria, is a combination of styles, centred upon an enormous fountain. It was created by King Ludwig II in the 1870s. The Eremitage at Bayreuth (right) was begun a century earlier but looks forward to 19th century Romanticism. Around the lake with its central fountain are a hermitage, a grotto and an artificial ruin.

Hidcote, in Gloucestershire, shows the influence of Lutyens and Jekyll, with its combination of picturesque planting and clipped hedges, brick paths and steps that re-introduce an element of classicism.

Ornamental originality reappeared with the advent of the Art Nouveau movement towards the end of the 19th century. Although its influence upon gardens was limited compared to its importance in other artistic spheres its effect can be seen in ironwork for gates and screens, in garden furniture and in some statuary, such as the series of bronze figures at Chirk Castle in Clwyd.

A movement which was to have far more influence upon English gardens was the Arts and Crafts, for out of it grew the partnership of Gertrude Jekyll and Edwin Lutyens. The style which they developed and practised with huge success combined plantsmanship and vernacular architecture to a most satisfying degree, as well as stressing the importance of a close integration of house and surrounding garden. Their work became the primary influence upon the development of English gardens through the 20th century and its influence can be clearly seen in some of the century's most celebrated gardens, such as Hidcote Manor in Gloucestershire and Sissinghurst Castle in Kent.

Since the days of the earliest Dutch and English settlers, the gardens of the United States have been strongly influenced by developments in Europe. At the same time gardens have evolved to demonstrate the size and diversity of the United States and the differences to be found in contrasting areas, as well as to reflect the character of the American people.

The first gardens were functional, growing vegetables and fruit for food. Once the settlers became more established and self-assured, flower gardening followed but there is little evidence of any sort of architectural or decorative ornament. During the 18th and early 19th centuries two gardens of considerable significance and influence were created by two of the country's foremost political figures, the first by George Washington at Mount Vernon, the second by Thomas Jefferson at Monticello. Both gardens were strongly influenced by the landscape style which had become established in England, but were adapted in a manner and to a scale that was distinctly American. There is still little architectural ornament other than small summerhouses and gazebos and the gardens' plans were essentially areas of flower beds and borders leading to more informal shrubberies linked by winding paths.

After the upheaval of the Civil War the return of peace to the United States ushered in a period sometimes known as the Country House Era, when the country's wealth and power made rapid advances. It was this generation of enormous wealth in the hands of private individuals which was to bring about an upsurge in ornamental gardening in many parts of the United States. The spirits of the Italian Renaissance and of Baroque France were emulated in impressive formal layouts dominated by pools, fountains and a rich variety of architectural ornament and smaller embellishments.

Shortly after the turn of the century one of the most spectacular American gardens was made at Longwood, Pennsylvania, for Pierre S. du Pont. Longwood's highlight is the enormous Fountain Garden where the complex series of jets rivals anything produced in France during the 17th century. The Italian Renaissance was most impressively revived at Villa Vizcaya, Florida, in the garden of James Deering made just before the beginning of the First World War. Here the whole design is Italian, with terraces and fountains and an abundance of imported 17th- and 18th-century statuary and urns.

Probably the most admired of these American gardens was one of the last to be created, at Dumbarton Oaks, Washington, DC. Owned by Mildred Barnes Bliss, Dumbarton Oaks was laid out between the wars and virtually all the design was by Beatrice Farrand. Here the Italian influence was most successfully incorporated into an American style which also revealed clear sympathy with English gardens and in particular with the work of Gertrude Jekyll. Dumbarton Oaks remains one of the truly outstanding gardens to have been made in the United States.

More than in almost any other country of the world, contemporary American gardens have shown a capacity to incorporate modern and abstract influences in both their overall design and the style of individual ornamental features. Free from the restrictions of a deeply entrenched historical tradition such as exists in all European countries, and aided by the manner in which original modern styles have been accepted in architecture, American garden designers have moved away from classical traditions more easily. As a result a truly individual American style of garden emerged during the post-war decades, no longer derivative from those European originals which provided the models for so much of the country's history.

Dumbarton Oaks, Washington DC, is among the most ambitious and successful gardens in the USA. It consists of a number of interrelated, small-scale spaces creating variety and surprise. Some elements are drawn from the European Arts and Crafts Movement, others (illustrated in colour) are purely American in inspiration.

II ORNAMENT AND ITS APPLICATION

George Plumptre

Architectural ornament·

THE FUNDAMENTAL STRUCTURE of any formal garden provides the basis for ornament and decoration. In addition, the fact that the creation of gardens has most often been motivated by the desire to achieve a picture of reassuring order and harmony has further ensured that architectural ornament – buildings providing outdoor rooms and thereby extending the house into the garden, enclosing walls, terraces, steps and stairways – has been of primary importance ever since the days of ancient Egypt and Mesopotamia.

This need for architecture in the garden has developed into almost limitless forms reflecting the tastes and styles of different periods. But if the appearances have changed, the principal requirements have remained constant. Today our garden buildings provide shade from the sun or shelter from cold and rain as they did for the ancients. They are places for meals or conversation, a destination to walk to from the house, a focal point or co-ordinating element in the garden's design.

Walls enclose gardens to give privacy and shelter, while the materials they are built of, the treatment of their tops, or the insertion of niches all provide the opportunity for ornament, as do the necessary openings such as gateways. Terraces are the logical means of constructing a garden on sloping terrain. By so creating a picture on different levels linked by stairways and with their retaining walls surmounted by balustrades – partly for safety, partly for decoration – they have produced some of the most spectacular gardens in history.

The functional limitations imposed upon such structural architectural features as walls and terraces means that their basic appearance has to follow a set pattern; it is superficial ornament and decoration which provide the variety. In the case of garden buildings no such limitations exist. They can satisfy any whim or folly which their builder cares to indulge in, as well as serving a practical purpose.

The design and construction of such buildings have often given leading architects the chance to leave their mark in gardens. Freed from the restrictions imposed upon them when working on houses, they have used garden architecture to display greater panache or originality than is usually permissible, allowing 'pure architecture' to call the tune. The results have been buildings of exceptional beauty and quality which have invested this sphere of garden ornament with considerable architectural importance.

Experienced architects of all ages and the men who have commissioned them have appreciated that such buildings need to convey a precise visual impact and to be equally effective whether viewed from a distance or from close quarters. Their conception has always demanded considerable skill. In some cases an over-ambitious edifice appears too dominant in a small garden while at the other extreme an insufficient building set at a distance to provide an eye-catcher or close a vista can fail in its intended purpose. Whether designed by an outstanding professional architect or a gifted amateur, garden buildings have always been most successful where the combination of their style, materials, proportions and position enhance their natural surroundings in an immediately satisfying manner.

Scotland has always been more open to French influence than England. The garden of
Drummond Castle, Perthshire, laid out in the mid-19th century, is French in its
formality, with its radiating paths focused on a 17th-century sundial. The house itself is
behind us, overlooking the parterre from the top of a steep slope.

The Gothic Temple at Bramham Park, Yorkshire, one of the many architectural features in this garden, which combines French formality with English naturalism.

Bramham Park in Yorkshire is the only large-scale formal landscape garden surviving in England from the first decade of the 18th century. The layout of the garden, which extends over 70 acres, was the work of Bramham's owner, Robert Benson, later created Lord Bingley, who also built the house. After his death in 1731 his only daughter Harriet married George Lane Fox, who became the second Lord Bingley. During the 1750s he commissioned the architect James Paine to design the Ionic temple which stands as the focal-point at the end of one of the garden's main vistas.

The delightful octagonal Gothic temple, which stands in the centre of a large sloping lawn, was built at the same time and is most likely to have also been the work of Paine. It serves as a summerhouse for the nearby bowling green, and was designed to be viewed from all sides, which accounts for its shape and symmetrical decoration. As an architect of houses Paine was a strict Palladian, for instance at Nostell Priory, Wardour Castle and the north front of Kedleston. But here at Bramham he indulges in a miniature digression into Gothic which survives as a rare gem among his work.

The garden of Goldney House at Clifton was laid out around the same time as Paine was working at Bramham and has a similar Gothic temple — circular rather than octagonal — at one end of its main terrace. A more original building, and one more representative of the spirit of the garden, whose most famous feature is its grotto, is the circular brick tower which stands behind the figure of Hercules with his club raised. The tower marks a break from the dominant architectural styles of the time and, although it was always designed to be intact, anticipates those artificial ruins that were later put up as eye-catchers by the leaders and devotees of the Picturesque movement.

The classical inspiration for an idealized landscape reached its peak in England around the middle of the 18th century and gardens were conceived principally as settings for temples and other buildings evoking the spirit of ancient Greece and Rome. Nowhere was this more true than at Stowe, which some critics accused of being so littered with buildings that any purpose in their position or relationship with each other was lost. Whatever the critics said, however, they could not dispute the quality and skill of the architects who worked at Stowe: Sir John

The Temple of British Worthies at Stowe, Buckinghamshire, is a curious hemicycle with niches containing busts of national heroes in the arts, politics and sciences, including King Alfred, Inigo Jones, Shakespeare and Newton.

The circular brick tower at Goldney House, Clifton, evokes the spirit of the Middle Ages, in contrast to the classical figure of Hercules with his club raised which stands in front of it.

Vanbrugh, James Gibbs and William Kent. It was Kent who gave Stowe its most original garden building in his Temple of British Worthies, which endowed the architectural style of ancient Rome with modern political significance.

The temple was planned as one of a group of three buildings, all designed by Kent, to stand in or near the Elysian Fields. Their interrelationship reflected the hostility of Stowe's owner, Lord Cobham, to Walpole and the other leading figures in English politics. The perfectly proportioned Temple of Ancient Virtue, to which all men aspired, contrasted with the Temple of Modern Virtue which was erected as a ruin. Looking upwards towards the Temple of Ancient Virtue are the sixteen busts in the niches of Kent's Temple of British Worthies, all portraying characters whom Cobham admired. The temple is designed as a curving *exedra*, severely classical and unlike anything else in English gardens.

Garden buildings occupying key positions and directing the eye to vistas can be among the most original of ornamental features. Left: the classical dovecot of Canon, Normandy (it is semicircular behind); the early 20th-century loggia at Nymans, Sussex; and the Japanese tea-house, also early this century, at Heale House, Wiltshire (the wooden construction, the thatched roof and the criss-crossing streams all derive from Japan). Above: gazebo and obelisks at Athelhampton, Dorset, a garden created in the 1890s and inspired by the 16th- and 17th-century manor house.

The long staircase of Drummond Castle, Perthshire, links the house with the large formal garden at a lower level. The architecture of Drummond belongs to the 17th century. The garden is a partial recreation of the original.

The centrepiece garden of the Villa Garzoni at Collodi consists of three terraces cut into a steeply sloping hillside, so that the staircases (here adorned with statues and decorative motifs) become the most prominent features.

The construction of terraces and the stairways or ramps to link them has often produced garden architecture at its most flamboyant and visually exciting. The combination of strong vertical elevations and contrasting horizontal perspectives is both stimulating in its strength and endlessly subtle in its possibilities for decorative ornament.

It was a combination ideally suited to the spirit of the Italian Renaissance with its invigorating blend of artistic quality and architectural and engineering prowess. At the same time it provided the means for capitalizing upon the often precipitous sites which were chosen for gardens. They seemed able to epitomize man's place in his natural surroundings and his ability to impose some sort of order upon those surroundings.

The work involved in the building of terraces, the moving of the earth and the erection of retaining walls, calls for considerable engineering skill, while the manner of designing the links between them needs equally great architectural imagination. As the Renaissance moved towards the Baroque the decorative and ornamental effects that could be achieved seemed almost limitless. Nowhere was the overall treatment more dramatic than at the Villa Garzoni. The centrepiece of the garden is the series of staircases which link the three main terraces and the parterre at the lowest level, where the outer sides of the staircase block are marked by statues set in niches.

By contrast, the sites chosen for most of the great French gardens were flat, or at least in terrain where the variation in level was so gradual that the effect is one of imposing grandeur rather than drama. Staircases were majestically wide with shallow risers. Walls were punctuated with balustrading as at Vaux-le-Vicomte (p. 53), to mark the control of large spaces and the ordered progression from one part of the garden to another.

An exception is the early 17th-century garden of the Château de Brécy in Normandy, shown on page 48, which was laid out in a series of five terraces ascending from the house and all richly decorated with Mannerist ornament. From the house the central staircases which link the terraces appear to ascend continuously to the monumental gateway that marks the garden's boundary with the countryside beyond.

There are very few garden sites in Britain which can rival the creations of the Italian Renaissance, but one which does is Powis Castle in Wales. Christopher Hussey described it as 'reproducing more nearly an Italian baroque terraced garden than any other surviving in England'. The date and architect of the terraces are both uncertain but it seems that they were laid out towards the end of the 17th century or early in the 18th and William Winde has been suggested as the possible architect.

The dramatic effect of the terraces with the castle perched above is enhanced by the colour of the red limestone of which both garden and castle are made. In true Italian style, the effect is as impressive from the bottom, when the vertical proportions are revealed, as from one of the terraces to the countryside beyond. Lead urns and statues decorating the balustrades of the terraces provide the foreground to these views.

A comparable site to Powis is that of Drummond Castle in Scotland where, again, the castle is perched at the top of a steep slope. At Drummond the main garden feature is the vast parterre which fills the flat rectangular area at the foot of the slope, the central section of which can be seen on page 41. Architecturally the most important question was how to link castle and parterre and how to treat the rocky hillside in between. Unlike Powis, where the hill is terraced with retaining walls, Drummond is left sloping. This accentuates the effect of the massive central staircases which rise from the parterre to the main terrace below the castle and on up to the castle courtyard.

At Powis Castle, in Wales, the inspiration is ultimately Italy, but the immediate model is said to have been St-Germain-en-Laye, near Paris. The garden occupies the side of a steep ridge. The terraces, up to seventy metres long, with their urns and statuary, were built in the late 17th or early 18th century. The dancing shepherds and shepherdesses could be by Van Nost.

Changes of level offer endless opportunities for staircases, balustrades and gates. The
17th-century Château de Brécy, in Normandy, consists of a series of terraces rising away
from the house and ending with these monumental gates. Opposite above: staircase of a
prince-bishop, at Würzburg, Bavaria, a typically German Baroque pattern punctuated by
statues. Right: Torosay Castle, Isle of Mull, by Robert Lorimer, early 20th century; and
Barton Manor, Isle of Wight, purchased by the Prince Consort in 1853.

Nineteenth-century Scotland was a place where the romanticism of the highlands and the baronial architecture of the castles occasionally combined to produce places of architectural fantasy. One such was Dunrobin Castle, where Sir Charles Barry was commissioned by the 2nd Duke of Sutherland to modernize the old castle. Like Drummond, Dunrobin sits on a hill overlooking its garden laid out below, but the treatment of the sloping terrace which leads down the hill, a series of stone balls surmounting the retaining wall, is surprisingly restrained compared to the castle and garden. Similar decoration can be seen on the balustrade at Haddon Hall in Derbyshire, shown on page 52.

The use of a balustrade to mark a boundary and at the same time provide an ornamental foreground for the view beyond was brought to perfection at Isola Bella on Lake Maggiore. When viewed from the surrounding water, the balustrades which surmount the retaining walls of the garden's terraces increase the dramatic upward thrust of the garden as a whole. Looking out from the garden, flanked by cypress trees and decorated with urns, they provide the necessary demarcation between the garden and the view beyond, while the spaces between their balusters give the impression that there is no break between garden and water.

Such masterly use of architecture and ornament was to be copied in later gardens created in the lakes of northern Italy, notably at the end of the 18th century, at Villa Balbianello on Lake Como and later at the 19th-century Villa San Remigio, also on Lake Maggiore. In both these gardens the urns of Isola Bella are replaced by statues, but the desired overall effect is the same.

Sir Charles Barry at Dunrobin Castle, Scotland, also went to the 17th century for inspiration. This long balustrade is given picturesque grandeur by the stone ball finials.

A balustrade at Isola Bella seems to mark a boundary between finite and infinite, preserving the medieval sense of the garden as an enclosed world, dedicated to happiness.

The ornamental styles of the Italian Renaissance were copied not only in Italy itself in later periods but all over Europe, not least in the terraced gardens of Victorian England. In some cases the Italian original was actually removed and re-erected in an English garden, as at Cliveden in Buckinghamshire, where the balustrades came from the Villa Borghese in Rome.

During the 20th century the creation of terraced gardens on a large scale has become prohibitively expensive and today they are virtually a thing of the past. One of the last to be made in England is at Port Lympne, created by Sir Philip Sassoon during the 1920s. The house is set on a hillside with a dramatic view of Romney Marsh beyond and Sassoon terraced much of the slope, giving it architectural continuity with the 135-step staircase which ascends through the garden.

'**Balustrades** are sometimes of real use in building, and at other times are merely ornamental,' wrote Sir Williams Chambers in 1759. 'Such as are intended for use . . . must always be nearly of the same height; never exceeding three feet and a half, nor ever being less than three. That so a person of an ordinary size may, with ease, lean over them, without being in danger of falling.' Opposite: Newby Hall, Yorkshire, late 19th century; Balmoral, mid-19th; Haddon Hall, Derbyshire, 17th century. Above: Vaux-le-Vicomte, mid-17th century. Right: Château-de-Brécy, Normandy, 17th century.

53

Structures such as the Temple of British Worthies are essentially ornamental, architectural statements and, in this case, part of an essay in classicism. Many other garden buildings have a primarily practical purpose, such as gazebos which, as their name suggests, were designed to provide an elevated view of a garden scene.

Westbury Court, as reconstructed by the National Trust during the 1960s, is the best surviving example of a formal Anglo-Dutch garden dating from the end of the 17th century. Because of the usually flat terrain in which Dutch gardens were made, gazebos were erected to provide elevated views of the formal parterres and canals. At Westbury the gazebo is positioned at the end of the garden's main formal canal and its perfectly proportioned vertical elevations contrast with the horizontal symmetry of the garden it overlooks. A loggia at ground level supports a first-floor room with three tall windows looking out over the main canal and across to the garden's second canal and formal parterre beyond. Surmounting the building is a cupola lantern whose extra height allows a view not only of the garden but also of the countryside leading to the River Severn beyond.

Westbury Court, Gloucestershire, laid out between 1694 and 1705, was clearly influenced by the Low Countries, with its combination of Dutch-style summer-house, clipped hedges and straight canal. The garden lay almost untouched for 250 years and has now been restored to its original condition.

The 'hameau' at Chantilly, like the slightly later one at Versailles, was a pseudo-rustic refuge for the princely family who lived in the château. Built in 1773, it is half-timbered with a thatched roof.

At Hall Place, Kent, the Victorian tea-pavilion playfully unites the rustic and the Gothic. The columns are tree-trunks, the tracery branches.

The gazebo at Westbury is a miniature version of the domestic architecture of William and Mary's reign. Such scaling down to a size suitable for a garden has been used to great effect, but whereas it is the orderliness and symmetry of classicism that has often dominated garden architecture, at times a quite different effect has been desired. The concept of the garden as a place of escape where man can be in close and informal contact with his natural surroundings has at times been accompanied by an appreciation of the countryside and its way of life and produced garden buildings which romanticize such a picture.

By the middle of the 18th century in France many people were reacting against the intense formality of court life of which the great formal gardens were a vivid image. During the 1770s a group of buildings called the Hameau ('hamlet') were added to the enormous existing gardens of Chantilly. They represented an idyllic scene of rustic life and anticipated by a few years the more famous Hameau made for Marie Antoinette near the Petit Trianon at Versailles. The buildings are black-and-white timbered and thatched and their inspiration was a hankering for peaceful simplicity.

A century after the Hameau was made at Chantilly, reaction against some of the excesses of English High-Victorian gardens combined with reaction against an increasingly industrial society to produce once again a desire for the rustic pleasures of life and for natural materials in preference to man-made ones. Out of this was born the Arts and Crafts Movement and buildings such as the tea pavilion at Hall Place in Kent appeared in many gardens. Its rough-hewn pillars and the patterns of branches filling the steeply pitched gables are absolutely characteristic of this Victorian idyll.

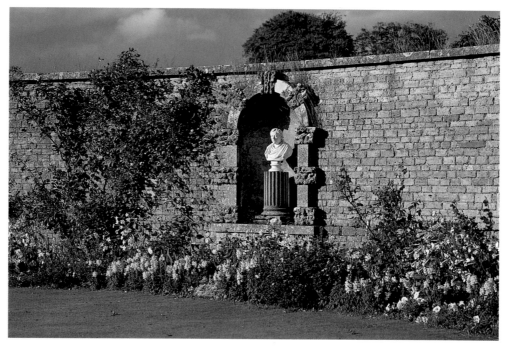

The wall shuts out the outside world and forms a setting for statuary and ornament. At his home, Iford Manor, Wiltshire (left), which he purchased in 1899, the architect Harold Peto used the wall to display part of his collection of antique sculpture, exactly as Cardinal Borghese had done at his Roman villa about 1620 (top). At Isola Bella (above left) the wall becomes a mosaic niche; and at Pusey House, Oxfordshire (above right), a real niche houses a bust on a pedestal, mid-20th century.

The loggia built by Sir Reginald Blomfield at Godinton Park, Kent, evokes classical Rome – as if a ruined temple or Pompeiian atrium had been converted into a garden colonnade.

In ancient classical and in Islamic gardens loggias and colonnades played an integral role. They could link house and garden or enclose a courtyard with a covered walkway, between whose arches and columns the central garden could be viewed. Alternatively, freestanding colonnades could be positioned so as to define but not divide space, providing an architectural screen between areas or strengthening the boundaries of a feature such as a pool or canal.

This use is ideally displayed at Hadrian's Villa near Tivoli where the remains include the curving colonnade around one end of the Canopus canal, its arches supported by Corinthian columns between which stand statues of heroic Greek figures (see page 60). In the picture of architectural harmony which the Canopus presents the colonnade is the perfect contrast to the arched *triclinium* at the far end of the canal.

During the Renaissance the use of colonnades was brought to its highest level by Bernini with the piazza in front of St Peter's Rome. It was demonstrated in more modest fashion in numerous gardens, following the example of Hadrian's Villa or deliberately conforming to what was read about Roman gardens. Loggias were often incorporated into the retaining walls of terraces in a manner which was later repeated in England at Powis Castle.

At the beginning of this century a number of English architects and garden designers strongly advocated a return to strict architectural formality in gardens and they looked to Italy for their inspiration. In some cases the movement produced single architectural features, such as the loggia at Nymans on page 44.

Elsewhere the result was complete Italian gardens, the most impressive being that at Hever Castle, made from 1905 for Lord Astor. The garden was planned to display his collection of antique statues and other sculpture; it terminated at one end in an impressive loggia, flanked by open colonnades and leading to a semi-circular piazza jutting out into the lake beyond.

The most influential book advocating a return to architectural formality in garden design was Sir Reginald Blomfield's *The Formal Garden in England*, published in 1892. Blomfield's ideas were best displayed at Godinton Park in Kent, where he worked on and off for many years from 1902. The Italian garden, confined within a small walled rectangle, was one of his last projects at Godinton and architecturally the most successful. At the far end from the entrance he built a loggia with classical figures between the columns, which is now romantically draped with wisteria.

Even more strongly Italian than the work of Blomfield were the architecture and garden design of his contemporary, Harold Peto. Peto designed a number of houses in the south of France where he made the incorporation of a loggia almost obligatory. But his fascination with Italian gardens and their contents is most clearly revealed in his own garden at Iford Manor, Wiltshire, which he created between the turn of the century and his death in 1933.

Capitalizing upon a site which sloped down from the house to the River Frome, he created a series of terraces and decorated them with the quantities of Italian statuary and other ornament which he had acquired. One of the most successful features is the colonnade which forms the centrepiece of the main terrace walk. An urn is set on a balustraded projection overlooking the broad steps which lead down to the formal round pool below. The effect is highly theatrical. Both mood and materials recall the style of the ancient world which Peto so admired.

Harold Peto's garden at Iford Manor, Wiltshire, incorporates genuine archaeological fragments. It is a personal statement, reflecting the owner's interests and preoccupations, and constituting a sort of private museum. The steepness of the site contributes an element of drama, rising from the River Frome in a series of terraces.

The columned screen had been a favourite Roman device for dividing and defining space.
Above: Hadrian's villa at Tivoli, accurately restored, is the source of many garden ideas.
Right: one of its progeny, Peto's screen at Iford Manor, Wiltshire, looking out over the
lush English landscape of the Frome Valley.

As important as the appearance of any freestanding piece of garden architecture is its position. Where this is part of a formal plan as within a walled enclosure, it is usually predetermined. At Montacute in Somerset, the breathtaking pair of garden pavilions echo the Elizabethan architecture of the house in both their style and material from across the main walled forecourt as they have done for four hundred years. But with many later gardens, where the design includes bold, outward-looking vistas, the scope is greatly increased by positioning a building or some more simple structure such as an obelisk either to close the vista or to lead the eye beyond the furthest point of vision.

This contrast is ideally illustrated by the two larger pictures on pages 64 and 65. At St Paul's Walden Bury in Hertfordshire one of the main vistas across the garden is closed by the classical temple built by Sir William Chambers which is positioned on the far side of the lake. The view extends for an impressive distance between beech hedges and closely planted taller trees across the water to the façade of the temple which marks the furthest boundary of the garden. At Château Canon in Normandy a quite different effect is achieved by the Chinese kiosk which also stands on the edge of the garden at the end of a long vista, but whose open design allows for the larger view beyond the garden's limits into the countryside beyond.

At Bramham Park in Yorkshire buildings provide the vital link between the two large areas of formal woodland garden. From the area immediately beyond the house the main vista, the Broad Walk, stretches right across the garden and out into open parkland. Beyond that the Round Temple – similar to the Temple of Ancient Virtue at Stowe – stands on the edge of the second area known as the Black Fen. Two hundred yards beyond, standing on the same line in the centre of the Black Fen, is the obelisk surmounted by an urn.

The obelisk at Kingston Lacy, in Dorset, is a genuine survival from ancient Egypt, of pink granite, discovered by William Bankes at Philae in 1815 and installed by him at his home Kingston Lacy in 1829.

Small-scale architecture in the form of festive summer-houses or gazebos were major features of Elizabethan and Jacobean gardens. These two pavilions at Montacute, in Somerset, are part of the original layout, later supplemented by Victorian additions in the same style.

The Column of Victory erected at Blenheim in 1727-30 is among the grandest of all garden ornaments. A fluted Doric column with a statue of the Duke of Marlborough on the top, it is both a ceremonial monument and a visual focus.

Because of their height obelisks have often been a favourite means of drawing the eye out of the garden to a distant point. The Romans acquired a considerable number from the ancient Egyptians and resited them, sometimes in their own gardens. But it was in England during the 18th century, when the divisions between garden and surrounding countryside were being swept away, that some of the most monumental obelisks – or columns such as the one at Blenheim Palace in Oxfordshire – were erected, often at a great distance from the house and almost inevitably commemorating some person, as did the one at Bramham. Two of the largest were those put up by Vanbrugh at Castle Howard in Yorkshire and by Kent at Holkham Hall in Norfolk.

Such 18th-century landscapes went beyond the realms of pure garden design as it had been understood in other periods, by virtue of the scale on which they were planned. Nonetheless, the siting of a single building or piece of architecture could still be of decisive importance in highlighting the significance of position. These basic principles were equally applicable in gardens of far more modest size and history has proved them to be fundamental to the success of architectural ornament.

*To **entice the eye** landscape architects employ endless variations on the theme of the vista, the gate, the entrance to spaces beyond. St Paul's Walden Bury, Hertfordshire, is a rare survival of an 18th-century formal garden, with allées cut through woods and ending at features like this classical temple designed by Sir William Chambers (opposite above). Below: entrance to a tunnel at Biddulph Grange, Staffordshire, a fantastic garden laid out in the 1850s by James Bateman; and one of the boundary gateways of Drummond Castle, Scotland. Above: a kiosk in the Chinese style at Canon, Normandy, late 18th century, arresting the eye but also tempting it onwards.*

Pergolas, treillage and ironwork

Because their function is to support plants, pergolas and treillage provide one of the closest links between ornament and horticulture. The practical importance of pergolas and their relatively simple basic structure accounts for the fact that they appeared in some of the earliest known gardens. They were used by the ancient Egyptians to support vines – an essential ingredient in any Egyptian garden – and to provide shaded but not completely enclosed walks. As gardens developed it is likely that they were also used to make the division between the productive 'kitchen' garden and the ornamental pleasure garden.

Most Egyptian pergolas were built of wood, though in some of the grandest gardens wooden uprights were replaced with brick ones. The rough-hewn wood of the earliest examples was eventually succeeded by more elegant carved pillars – sometimes painted – and it would not be too fanciful to suggest that an Egyptian vine pergola would look very similar to the one at Chenonceaux, except that they would not have been curved.

The basic design and usage of the pergola has not changed during the thousands of years since then. Therefore when the potager at Villandry was restored by Doctor Joachim Carvallo at the beginning of this century, he faithfully supplied the wooden vine pergolas which play an integral role in the overall design (see page 76) as they would have done in the 18th-century original.

While a variety of materials has been used for the uprights or piers, the beams forming the framework across the top have virtually always been made of wood. Because they are designed to support plants which will provide a decorative element, pergolas have rarely been highly carved or ornamented. Instead the preference has been for simple symmetry and strength.

The most important step in the evolution of the pergola came when it was no longer seen as a means of supporting only vines, but any other suitable climbing plant. It proved to be the ideal medium to unite the horticultural skills of Gertrude Jekyll and the architectural ones of Edwin Lutyens, as is shown in a number of the gardens where they worked together.

Writing in her book *Garden Ornament*, Gertrude Jekyll expressed surprise that it had taken so long for the varied potential of the pergola to be appreciated. '. . . And though its original purpose was the support of vines only, yet it need not have taken centuries for us to perceive how conveniently it could be adapted to flowering plants of climbing habit, or to see how its structure could be suited to every kind and degree of gardening, from the highest expression of architecture . . . to the simplest erection of posts or even poles in the garden of an English cottage.'

Gertrude Jekyll goes on to give precise details as to how, in her opinion, a pergola should best be constructed, details which she and Lutyens were to put into practise to such effect. It is arguable that they never bettered one of their earliest collaborations, at Hestercombe in Somerset, where the pergola some 70 metres long encloses one side of the main garden. It is representative in every detail: the piers are built of local stone, the beams are of oak, those going across slightly cambered for, in Gertrude Jekyll's own words, 'the upward curve, if even quite slight, gives a satisfying look of strength.' The pergola supports pink and white roses; below, the planting is blue, yellow, grey and green. The overall effect is a consummate balance of horticulture and architecture.

Two examples of the imaginative use of pergolas. Opposite: Biltmore, North Carolina, a garden made for the Vanderbilt family in the 1890s by the great landscape architect Frederick Law Olmsted. Above: a Lutyens pergola at Hestercombe, Somerset, of 1906. The heavy stone piers and oak beams evoke the simple vernacular tradition.

Transparent wrought iron *marks a stop but also signals further progress, while at the same time intriguing the eye with its delicate shapes. Robert Bakewell's craftsmanship at Melbourne Hall, Derbyshire (left), of 1710, competes with the spider's web in delicacy (see p.109). Whatton House, Leicestershire (below), introduces the Art Nouveau curves of about 1900. A gate of the Queen Anne period at Norton Conyers, Yorkshire (opposite), uses heraldic ironwork to lead into the kitchen garden.*

Decorative wrought iron can be a work of art in its own right, reaching a peak of sophistication in the 17th and 18th centuries. Right: the Birdcage Arbour made by Robert Bakewell at Melbourne Hall, Derbyshire.

A Rococo gate at Würzburg, Germany, 18th century. Asymmetrical, fanciful, tense with contained energy, this masterfully executed design seems as alive as the plants that cluster near it.

After wood the material which has been used most frequently to support plants is iron. Whether as wrought iron or later as cast iron, its combination of malleability and strength makes it ideal for supporting frameworks, while its greater resistance to weather makes it far longer-lasting than wood. It is the workable nature of the metal which has enabled it to be used to such decorative effect. Historically ironwork is more important in ornamental forms such as gates, screens and balustrades than in the more practical capacity of providing a supporting framework.

Ironwork was used extensively in Italian Renaissance gardens and later in France, most frequently in gates, balustrading and railings. Usually it was painted black but in French gardens such as Versailles it was often given great richness by the addition of gilded ornamental details. It was in England, however, that the working of iron was brought to its highest level of skill and beauty during a period which began at the end of the 17th century with the work of Jean Tijou. Tijou was a French Huguenot who came to England shortly after the arrival of William and Mary and it was for these royal patrons that he produced his most exquisite work, in particular for Hampton Court.

The technique which Tijou employed was *repoussé*, the hammering and shaping of flat sheets of metal into decorative relief. His greatest creation for Hampton Court was the Fountain Screen which forms the riverside boundary of the garden and consists of twelve enormous linked panels. Equally sumptuous are his gateways leading out from the formal parterre garden to the two side avenues of the *patte d'oie* laid out for Charles II in the style of Le Nôtre, and the balustrade which overlooks the canal along the main central avenue.

Tijou was important not only for the work he produced but also the influence he had on what became a thriving school of English ironwork. He employed a number of apprentices who absorbed and perpetuated his techniques. The most outstanding of this next generation was Robert Bakewell from Derbyshire. If Bakewell did not actually study under Tijou he was profoundly influenced by him and aspired to the same level of ornamental skill. For much of his career Bakewell worked from a smithy in the village of Melbourne near Derby and his masterpiece was produced for the nearest important garden, Melbourne Hall. The Birdcage Arbour stands on the far side of a circular pool as the focal-point of the main sweep of garden down the slope from the front of the house. The richness of the overall effect is heightened by the fact that some of the details are picked out with gilding and coloured paint.

The widespread introduction of cast iron during the 19th century meant that patterns or sculptural forms could be reproduced at will. As a result the originality and quality – if not the decorativeness – of most ironwork declined from the zenith it had achieved at the beginning of the 18th century. Occasional modern influences appeared as in the Art Nouveau gate at Whatton in Leicestershire, shown on page 68, but by and large imitation became the order of the day and the achievements of the past were heavily relied upon for designs and styles.

During the 20th century, if ironwork has become an expensive luxury in most gardens and something of a dying art in terms of original craftsmanship, it is still important as an element of garden ornament. And it retains its usefulness as a support for climbing plants.

Detail of the ornamental screen made for the Fountain Garden at Hampton Court by Jean Tijou, who introduced new standards of technical quality and of design to England in the late 17th century. His work is also to be seen in St Paul's Cathedral.

Trelliswork *(or 'treillage'), like ironwork, defines space without enclosing it. It also provides support for plants. The rose arbour at Beauforest House, Oxfordshire (above), stands at a junction of four paths and provides an open focal-point; at Holker Hall, Cumbria (opposite above), trelliswork pillars give privacy to a seat and provide a frame for climbing roses. Opposite below: Kent's trelliswork gazebo and seat at Rousham, Oxfordshire, 18th century; and the bright red Japanese bridge at Heale House, Wiltshire, a cultural transplant of early this century.*

If pergolas have changed little throughout many thousands of years, treillage, or trellis-work, has had infinitely varied application. In medieval gardens it was often referred to as 'carpenters' work' and was used to provide low decorative fencing around flowerbeds, or framework for arbours or shaded walks. Treillage is, by definition, made of wood, and has remained 'carpenters' work'. But at certain times it has gone further than that and developed into a highly ornate and skilful art. The earliest significant examples appeared in French gardens of the late 16th and early 17th centuries.

The importance of treillage in French gardens was clearly demonstrated when Pierre le Nôtre, the first of the illustrious family of gardeners, applied to be accepted as a master-gardener in the Paris Guild. His *chef-d'oeuvre* was a series of designs for treillage. One of the few garden designs by his more famous grandson, André, which survives in engraved form shows a plan for a parterre overlooked from one end by a curving portico of trellis-work, complete with columns and a central pediment.

One of the most widespread uses of trellis-work was in *berceaux* or series of arbours linked by screens enclosing small gardens within a larger design. An ideal example was the Maison de Sylvie at Chantilly designed by Claude Desgots around 1670, where the building at one end looked on to a small formal garden completely enclosed by *berceaux*. Chantilly also boasted a most elaborate trellis-work building in the Temple de l'Amour, whose open arches, divided by columns surmounted by trellis-work urns, supported a large dome and cupola above.

Treillage continued to be extremely popular in French gardens throughout the 18th and 19th centuries. A notable example in England can be seen in the pair of small trellis-work pavilions enclosing garden seats which William Kent designed for Rousham, one of which is shown on page 73. It was employed in characteristically ambitious style in a number of late-Victorian and Edwardian gardens where long colonnades ending in pavilions or screens with classical columns were constructed. Harold Peto was one leading garden architect who used such trellis-work designs in a number of his gardens, such as Easton Lodge in Essex and Bridge House in Surrey.

The Temple de l'Amour at Chantilly, near Paris, was treillage at the farthest possible remove from rustic traditions. Everything here, even the urns, was made of wooden trellis-work.

The simple trellis arbour at Villandry is a faithful copy (1906-24) of what would have existed in the 17th century.

Perspective trellis-work has been a popular device in France for giving interest to a blank wall and suggesting further vistas beyond. This example at the Château de Brécy is particularly elaborate.

Such grandiose designs have virtually disappeared in most 20th-century gardens and treillage is more often put to its original use of supporting plants or providing the framework for arbours over which plants are trained, as in the restored garden at Villandry. In small gardens it can be used most effectively as *trompe l'oeil* perspectives set in a boundary wall, thereby seeming to lengthen the vista. Indeed one of the attractions of trellis-work is that it is supremely adaptable, as effective in small as in large gardens, whether making a single modest pillar up which climbers are trained or a larger white-painted rose arbour as the centrepiece of a formal layout.

The pergola is an extension of trellis, a framework upon which a tunnel of vegetation can be created, and leading the eye into the distance. This pergola at Villandry, Indre-et-Loire (left), actually supports vines, though its 18th-century geometry, restored in 1902-24, is part of a particularly sophisticated design. Schwetzingen (above) represents an interesting German variant, late 18th century.

LES III. FONTAINES.

Water, fountains and grottoes

It is in their use of water and its association with architecture and sculpture that garden designers have reached their highest levels of aesthetic and visual achievement. For water imparts that element of the intangible, something that is neither man-made nor horticultural; a certain magic incorporating the interplay of movement and repose, of light and shade, of sound and silence. Throughout history writers have attempted to grasp and record why it is that water so influences the mood of a garden. Osbert Sitwell wrote about the Villa Lante: 'But the soul of the garden is in the blue pools which, by some strange wizardry of the artist, to stair and terrace and window throw back the undimmed azure of the Italian sky.'

In the hot countries where gardens originated the need for water was practical, to provide irrigation. Nothing grew without water and as rainfall was not sufficient man had to guarantee the water supply himself. From this primitive requirement has developed a certain spirituality associated with water which has permeated religion, philosophy and aesthetics and whose expression has been most satisfying in gardens. Man soon discovered that as well as feeding the plants and trees in their gardens water provided coolness and diffused harsh sunlight in a manner which was equally refreshing for his own body and mind.

Water has countless other guises apart from its practical importance and spiritual significance. In fountains and jets it is alive and frenetic, in cascades it is full of vigour which at times threatens to break out of the limits imposed, in canals and pools it is contemplative and, when spread over a large area, majestically impressive. At the same time it has produced a host of associated garden ornaments and architectural features: carvings, statues or other sculpture to adorn fountains; masks and gargoyles to spout from walls; bridges to cross small streams or great lakes; and grottoes to provide the opportunity for any imaginable excursion into the realms of mythology and fantasy.

The first gardens where the integral importance of water went beyond the purely practical were those of the ancient Persians from whom emerged the gardens of Islam. For to the Muslim water was always scarce and therefore to be treasured and celebrated. He did so in his garden and delighted in any expression of the life-giving element. The fundamental design was a cross of water channels or canals which produced the traditional *chahar bagh* — literally four gardens. At the junction of the canals the focal-point of the garden was a building or a water supply tank, always filled to the brim to represent paradise overflowing with water.

Islamic gardens established the canal as the most satisfying water feature within a symmetrical overall plan. Such rectangular sheets of water can give a feeling of serenity to a garden and at the same time add an extra dimension to the harmony of the picture through the reflections they provide. This effect was brought to its highest expression in Islamic gardens at the Taj Mahal at Agra, the tomb built in the middle of the 17th century by Shah Jahan for his wife Mumtaz Mahal.

'Les Trois Fontaines' at Versailles — one of the most spectacular of the sequences devised by Louis XIV's 'fontainier' Girard. The Versailles waterworks were always more striking in intention than in reality because of the insoluble problem of providing enough water at the right pressure.

Water is the single most vital element in gardens, and from ancient Mesopotamia to modern America its functional importance has been signalled by its aesthetic role. At the 16th-century Villa Lante, Bagnaia, the most exquisite of all Italian gardens, an ornamental pool (left) enriched with sculptures and balustrades lies beneath a series of cascades. Above and below: gushing water in two rival gardens of late 16th-century Italy; a stone mask in Cardinal Alessandro Farnese's 'giardino segreto' at Caprarola, designed by Vignola, and the Fountain of the Dragons in Ippolito d'Este's at Tivoli, by Ligorio.

Whitfield, Herefordshire: here the fountain provides a centrepiece to the lawn in front of the house, where the eye pauses before going on to the landscape beyond.

At the Villa Lante the climax of the garden is the water parterre at the lowest level, a square of water divided into four pools surrounding the central circular fountain. The genius of the conception lies in the contrast of the silent, motionless pools and constant sound and activity of the water flowing from the fountain.

Few gardens can emulate the architectural perfection of the Villa Lante, but the relationship between formal pool and central fountain has been one of the most widespread and successful features of water in gardens of all periods of history, from early Islam onwards. At all times the appeal has been the balance between repose and motion, when the quiet surface of a pool is brought to life by the constant play of a fountain.

In some cases the fountain is left unadorned as a jet or falls into a simple basin. At Whitfield in Herefordshire the modest pool and fountain in front of the house provides an ideal foreground without detracting from the magnificent view out to the park. At Athelhampton in Dorset, the main axis of the garden laid out in the 1890s stretches through three contrasting pools and fountains, from the Yew Garden at one end to the rectangular pool in the Private Garden shown on page 101.

In contrast to such reticence is the richness of fountains incorporating statues or larger sculptural groups, as at the Villa Lante, and it was during the Italian Renaissance that such fountains achieved a pinnacle of artistic quality. The statues were made by the great craftsmen of the day and provided models that have been copied ever since. Among the most reproduced is the figure of Mercury, originally made for the garden of the Villa Medici in Rome by Giambologna; a copy of it at Syon House in Middlesex is shown on page 88.

If the fountains of the Italian Renaissance are unsurpassed for their quality, those of Baroque France, in particular at Versailles, represent a peak of sumptuousness. As with all the statuary at Versailles, the figures and groups which form the centrepieces of the various basins are part of the overall conception. Their appearance and position are determined by their relationship with the dominant figure —

Apollo the Sun God. He takes centre-stage in the group in the Bassin d'Apollo. As is shown in the Dragon Fountain on page 85, one important characteristic of the sculptural groups is that they appear to lie dormant in the surrounding still water of their pools, until brought to life by the jets of their fountains.

Although no subsequent garden could boast a more lavish array of fountain sculpture than Versailles, its riches were aspired to by both contemporary and later garden makers all over Europe. In Germany, where the end of the Thirty Years War in 1648 marked the beginning of a period of wonderful productivity in both architecture and garden design by the various princes, the French model was both admired and, at times, competed with. At Herrenhausen in Hanover, the Grosser Garten or 'Great Garden' created by Sophie, the wife of Duke Ernst August, was one of the outstanding German Baroque gardens. The centrepiece of the main parterre was a large basin surrounded by smaller basins with central fountains.

Water at its most formal is exemplified in such gardens as Herrenhausen in Hanover, where the rigidly symmetrical layout with its intersecting paths, is centred on two round ponds with fountains.

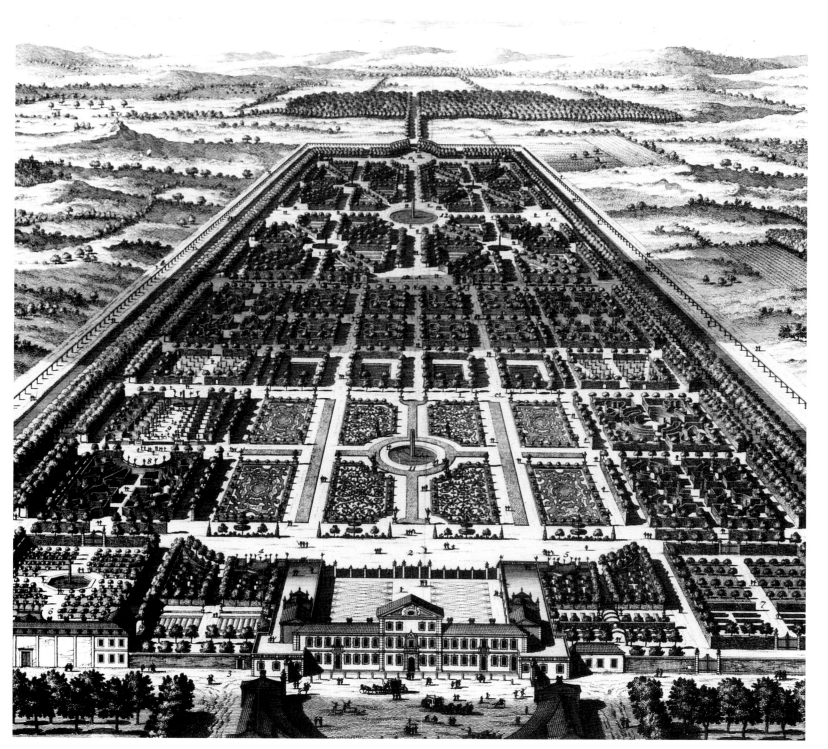

Nowhere else in Europe was water used as exuberantly as in Renaissance Italy,
although at Versailles (right) it was used on an unprecedented scale in the huge canals and
basins, such as the one containing the Dragon Fountain shown here. Far smaller in scale is
the Dutch-inspired T-shaped canal at Westbury Court, Gloucestershire, a William and
Mary garden of the 1690s.

Vaux-le-Vicomte has fewer fountains than Versailles but its use of water is in some ways subtler. Here the whole château is reflected in the formal pool half way along the main vista.

The use of such canals or formal *bassins* of water reached its zenith in French gardens of the 17th century. In contrast to the vigorous use of water in Italian gardens, in France the primary objective was undisturbed grandeur, as was achieved by André le Nôtre at Vaux-le-Vicomte. While Le Nôtre was later to work on a larger scale at Versailles, he did not improve upon the genius of his overall concept at Vaux-le-Vicomte. From the formal moat which surrounds the elevated platform on which the château itself is built the size and position of the various *bassins* throughout the gardens are unerringly harmonious and in proportion with the overall plan. The symmetry is extended to the reflections which they give so that, for instance, the Miroir d'Eau on the central axis is positioned so as to reflect exactly the complete façade of the château.

The expanses of water are also used to render the various changes in level through the gardens almost imperceptible. Where the changes are deliberately exploited, water is used to confirm the rise or fall, most dramatically in the Grand Canal which forms the main cross-axis. The canal extends for nearly a kilometre across the garden and its awe-inspiring appearance is accentuated by its sunken position which conceals it from view as one approaches from the château.

Le Nôtre's grandiose designs had a strong influence in Germany which was clearly evident in the garden of Schleissheim in Bavaria, made by the Elector Max Emanuel. He had visited Versailles often enough to collect much information about the gardens and Schleissheim was dominated by the series of canals. At the same time canals were integral in Dutch gardens. Their use was more modest, reflecting the conditions and attitudes prevalent in the small Protestant, mercantile republic which were quite different from those in absolutist France. Ideally suited to the flat countryside of the Netherlands, canals in Dutch gardens evolved from the expertise gained in the construction of such waterways for drainage, together with a desire for orderly and subdued classicism in garden design.

English gardens towards the end of the 17th century were influenced by both French and Dutch styles. The contrast between them is well illustrated by comparing the impressive Long Canal at Hampton Court, added by Charles II who aspired to the grandeur of Le Nôtre's work, and the smaller, more intimate Anglo-Dutch garden of Westbury Court in Gloucestershire.

As originally laid out at the end of the 17th century, Westbury Court's major feature was the main canal stretching away from the Dutch-style gazebo or summer-house. During the 18th century a second T-shaped canal was added parallel to the first. By this time, however, the formal style of gardening that had been used at Westbury was becoming unfashionable and by the end of the century the Picturesque Movement and its desire to recreate the natural landscape had brought about the demise of virtually all 17th-century formal gardens in England.

It was not until the 20th century that canals or similar formal pieces of water reappeared in English gardens. The work of Harold Peto at Buscot Park, Oxfordshire, Thomas Mawson at Little Onn Hall in Staffordshire and Reginald Blomfield at Godinton Park in Kent, shown in the illustrations on pages 96 and 97 are all examples from this period. At Garsington Manor in Oxfordshire Lady Ottoline Morrell created the Italian garden where the temple and classical statues look out over the still waters of a square pool.

Hampton Court is the closest that England comes to Versailles. But while the long canal with its main vista remains in all its impressive length, reeds, water-lilies and trees have softened the original formality into something more picturesque.

Domestic classicism: Lady Ottoline Morrell's garden at Garsington, Oxfordshire, shows how grandeur can be achieved on a relatively small scale. It is divided into a number of self-contained parts, one of which is a formal pool with an island in the middle and a classical temple at one end.

Moving water imparts life to the garden. Here again, the inspiration comes from
Renaissance and Baroque Italy, whether the water flows downwards in the form of
'water-staircases' or is flung upwards from the jets of fountains. Above left: the 'catena
d'aqua' in the Casino garden of the Farnese Palace, Caprarola, with the Casino at the top
guarded by giants. Above right: two English fountains, at Syon House, near London,
using a copy of Giambologna's Mercury; and Holker Hall, Cumbria. The modern water-
staircase (opposite) is also at Holker.

During the Italian Renaissance ingenuity and engineering transformed the use of water in gardens to spectacular effect. Features such as pools or basins and fountains became essential to the development of gardens. The Italians inherited certain traditions from their predecessors and handed on others to their successors. But the spirit of the Renaissance was represented by a vigour and ebullience which were the unique hallmarks of the period.

This vitality was to produce impressive or delightful water effects in the majority of gardens made after the beginning of the 16th century, but in one garden, the Villa d'Este at Tivoli, they produced an unrivalled display. Architect of both villa and garden was Pirro Ligorio, who was, with Vignola, one of the most distinguished garden architects of the Renaissance. At the Villa d'Este he combined his great knowledge of the architecture of ancient Rome with startling originality, creating a garden which was literally alive with water.

It was laid out between 1560 and 1575 on a steep hillside below the villa. Ligorio created a series of magnificent terraces up the slope joined by a series of stairways and ramps along a central axis. The terraces were lavishly decorated with statuary, much of which was removed by Ligorio's patron, Cardinal Ippolito d'Este, from nearby Hadrian's Villa.

The Terrace of One Hundred Fountains at the Villa d'Este cuts across the main descent of the garden like an emphatic punctuation mark. Here is water in every shape, gushing into the air, cascading over rocks and flowing from spouts into long basins.

Another view of the Villa d'Este garden. At the back, a fantastic Mannerist pavilion covered in grotesque sculpture; then a series of terraces with surging jets of water; at the bottom, a classical statue veiled behind a cascade of water; and in the foreground, water at rest.

Water was diverted from a nearby river and brought to the garden by a combination of aqueducts and conduits which was a considerable feat of engineering in itself. Once a constant supply of sufficient quantity was guaranteed, the water was deployed throughout the gardens to bring it to life in a series of breathtaking displays. Some of the most monumental fountains, such as the Fountain of the Organ, were positioned in enclosed garden rooms at the ends of terraces, where the water rose in great plumes and then cascaded away through a series of ponds. The Fountain of the Dragons shown on page 81 forms the centrepiece of two curving stairways rising from one level of the garden to the next where the Terrace of One Hundred Fountains stretches across the garden. Right along the length of the terrace small single jets in three levels spout between stone eagles and *fleurs de lys* – the arms of the Este family.

The water was used to produce noises and to activate *automata*, so that the Fountain of the Organ played a note, the Dragon Fountain roared and in the Fountain of the Owl small birds moved and an owl hooted. It also satisfied the Renaissance sense of humour and enjoyment of practical jokes in the form of *giochi d'aqua* – water games – which, by means of concealed hydraulic devices, surprised unsuspecting visitors in a number of ways, usually by soaking them with a sudden deluge.

Over and above the bravado of the individual features at Villa d'Este, the overwhelming impression recorded by most observers was the sheer quantity of water in perpetual motion which seemed to be constantly celebrating the spirit of the age.

A cascade is the most dramatic way of marking a change in level, an effect that can be increased by sculpture or the imitation of natural features. Above: detail of one of the cascades at Wilhelmshöhe, in Germany, begun in 1701. Left and opposite: two views of Courances, near Paris, a 17th-century garden making notable use of water; it was restored in the 19th century and new elements were added, including this pool with water-spout and nymph.

The gardens of the Neapolitan royal palace at Caserta rival those of Versailles in scale, though not in the diversity of their features. The top of the cascade is over a mile from the palace, falling steeply over rocks to end in a pool which contains life size statues of Actaeon surprising Diana and her nymphs, transformed into a stag and torn to pieces by her dogs.

The Villa d'Este was conceived by Ippolito d'Este to compete with the palazzo being built at the same time by his adversary Cardinal Alessandro Farnese at nearby Caprarola. Farnese's architect for both the palace and gardens was Vignola. At some distance from the monumental palace Vignola devised a small casino garden as a place of seclusion, whose outstanding feature was the *catena d'aqua* shown on page 88, one of the most delightful water effects to be found in any Italian garden. Water flows out of a basin and down the centre of a ramp where it is contained in a narrow channel with stone sides carved into interlinking scrolls. Vignola repeated the device at the Villa Lante, giving it visual significance for his patron, Cardinal Gambara, by designing the scrolled sides of the channel to be the limbs of crayfish – the cardinal's symbol.

These *catene d'aqua* were rare refinements of the cascade, to which the terrain of Italian gardens was ideally suited. Elsewhere the treatment is more energetic, as at the Villa Garzoni where the water flows out of the pool shaded by trees at the top of the garden and rushes down the central cascade towards the three main terraces. The cascade at Villa Garzoni is occasionally referred to as a water staircase, of which a more obvious example is at the Villa Aldobrandini in Frascati, where the water flows down eight steps towards the garden's great semi-circular water theatre.

The cascades of Italian gardens were widely copied throughout Europe, at times on an almost excessively lavish scale. At the beginning of the 18th century both the gardens of La Granja at Segovia in Spain and the Peterhof outside Leningrad in Russia were planned around marble cascades and later in the century the longest series of cascades in Europe was created at Caserta near Naples. Among the most ambitious schemes, which was never completed, was that for Wilhelms-höhe at Hessen in Germany, conceived by Landgrave Karl of Hesse-Kassel. Inspired by what he had seen in Italy – notably the Villa Aldobrandini – he planned a series of cascades that would drop through some 200 metres over a distance of a kilometre.

In England the only example of a cascade on the grand scale is at Chatsworth in Derbyshire where the water appears from the superb Cascade House built by Thomas Archer. In France they were equally unusual and both the style of gardening and the undulating rather than precipitous terrain advocated the use of water in a less energetic manner. A perfect example of the adaption of the cascade to the French style was created at Courances in Essonne, where the original 17th-century garden was restored at the beginning of the 20th century.

The major features of the garden at Courances are the various basins and canals whose motionless surfaces emphasize the unusual clarity of the water which comes from natural springs. Where the water moves it does so in a leisurely and controlled manner in sympathy with the overall mood of repose. Down one gentle slope are a series of shallow cascades with unusually long steps so that the flow of water is a quiet and graceful progress from one level to the next. The single cascade which pours into the basin below the stone nymph shown on page 93 is similarly restrained.

Chatsworth, Derbyshire: looking from the top of the cascade downwards towards the house, which can be glimpsed at the bottom on the right. The cascade was built in 1694 by Grillet, a pupil of Le Nôtre.

The geometry of water: *in these gardens the effect is one of tranquillity rather than excitement. Above: two views, looking in opposite directions, of Harold Peto's water garden at Buscot Park, Oxfordshire, 1904-11. The water descends very gradually towards a lake, the end of the vista marked by a temple on the further bank. Left: Kent's octagonal 'Cold Bath' at Rousham, Oxfordshire, part of the 'Watery Walk' through trees, 1740. Right: Little Onn, Staffordshire, by the prolific gardener Thomas Mawson, around 1900; two octagonal pools linked by a canal. Far right: Godinton Park, Kent, another Edwardian essay in the Italianate style by Reginald Blomfield.*

The symbolism of water spouting from satyr-like faces goes back to the ancient world, where every stream had its presiding deity. Above: a fountain in the grounds of the Villa Borghese, Rome. Below: Buontalenti's grotto in the Boboli Gardens, Florence, decorated not only with strange petrified figures and trees but also (up to 1908, when they were removed to the Academia) with Michelangelo's unfinished slaves, made for the tomb of Julius II.

On the far side of the basin from the nymph and cascade at Courances, the water pours down to the canal on the next level from the mouths of stone dolphins, one of which is shown on page 92. Such spouts, or masks, which ensure a measured flow of water, have often been integral parts of water gardens, either as the best ornamental means of diverting water from one level to another, or incorporated into fountains, or set in a wall. On page 81 a stone mask at the Palazzo Farnese, Caprarola, is shown emitting jets of water from both nose and mouth. In many Italian gardens the most regularly used 'face' for water spouts was Bacchus, who appears at the Villa Reale. At the Villa d'Este water spouts from the two breasts of a stone sphinx in the centre of the Terrace of the Hundred Fountains, while elsewhere in the garden is the many-breasted figure of Diana of Ephesus.

Such spouting figures and masks were used extensively in one of the most ancient structural features associated with water, the grotto. The two sources of inspiration for the grotto were natural caves which provided water sources and more architectural nymphaeums which celebrated water nymphs. They provided the opportunity for the most imaginative, at times fantastic decoration and ornament, with curving walls and ceilings covered with artificial stalactites, stucco-work of designs of shells, all constantly dripping with water.

References to grottoes in ancient Greek and Roman literature, their mythological significance and the opportunities they presented for elaborate ornament all gave them great appeal during the Italian Renaissance. Most important gardens had at least one grotto. One of the most impressive was made at the Medici Villa at Castello. A pillared entrance in the upper wall of the main garden led into the extensive grotto which soon became famous for its collection of life-size animals and birds all spouting water from various parts of their bodies.

Pommersfelden is one of many German Rococo grottoes with lively statuary and ingenious shellwork. Particularly popular in German and Austrian grottoes were waterworks that could soak unwary guests from concealed jets in the floor and ceiling.

Admiration for Italian gardens as well as their capacity for decoration and illusion ensured that grottoes continued to be incorporated into European gardens throughout the 17th and 18th centuries. Their romantic potential greatly appealed to garden makers in Germany, where highly ornate grottoes were made at Wilhelmshöhe near Kassel and later during the 18th century, at Rococo gardens such as Veitshochheim in Bavaria.

Continued interest in classical literature in England during the 18th century partly accounts for the popularity of grottoes. Alexander Pope seems to have initiated it in his garden at Twickenham. Once such an important arbiter of taste had shown the way it was inevitable that his lead would be widely followed. An outstanding grotto was made by Henry Hoare at Stourhead, a decisive part of the imaginary landscape inspired by the *Aeneid* which is the theme of the planned journey around the garden. Inside the grotto the control of water, whereby natural springs are channelled to emerge in a cascade below the statue of a sleeping nymph or from the urn of the river god, combines with the artistic quality of the statues themselves. One of the most elaborate grottoes was made by Charles Hamilton at Painshill in Surrey, whose fantastic decoration no doubt owed something to Hamilton's fondness for *chinoiserie*.

Although grottoes have virtually disappeared as a form of garden ornament their importance for many centuries was considerable, not least because their potential for decoration and for architectural ingenuity was enhanced by an air of mystery – a combination that has been fundamental to the use of water in gardens throughout history.

The focal point of a pool is often a fountain, equally effective on any scale. The huge basin above, supported on giant claws, is at the Villa Medici at Castello. That on the right is at Montacute, in Somerset. The gazebo in the background is part of the late 16th-century layout; the balustraded pond and fountain were added in the late 19th. The bronze figure at the Villa Borghese (left) is also a modern addition in an ancient setting. Right: two more Edwardian evocations of an earlier age, at Athelhampton, Dorset, and Duntreath Castle, Scotland.

'Lion attacking a Horse' by Peter Scheemakers,
made in 1740 for the garden at Rousham,
Oxfordshire. Such subjects – serving to remind
the spectator of the violent and untamed side of
nature which civilization controls and renders
harmless – have been an intermittent feature of
gardens throughout history.

Statuary

The artistic quality and position of the *Lion attacking a Horse* at Rousham make it a consummate example of the use of statuary in the garden. It was made in 1740 by Peter Scheemakers, a Dutchman who came to England c. 1730 and became one of the foremost sculptors of the 18th century. Copied from an ancient Roman model, the sculpture stands at the far end of the large bowling-green in front of the house, its dramatic impact and vitality heightened from this viewpoint by the manner in which it is silhouetted as the ground drops steeply away immediately beyond.

Such all-round excellence, the ideal harmony between subject matter, materials, situation and desired effect, has been the elusive goal ever since statues and other sculpture were first used as ornament in gardens. Until the end of the 18th century they either had religious or philosophical significance or important allegorical meaning, or they represented the desire to illustrate — in an idealized fashion — man and other animate objects in their natural surroundings. For the last two centuries, as ornamental gardening has become increasingly derivative, their primary importance has been to provide decorative effect, to enhance and enliven the architectural formality of a garden, or to provide the foil to a planting scheme.

In ancient gardens their appearance was motivated by reverence and the urge to glorify superior beings. The Egyptians adorned their gardens with their deities and sphinxes, while the ancient Greeks put up statues of their gods and heroes. The subject matter was similar in Roman gardens, with the important development that the choice and position of statuary was carefully considered as part of an overall design, as illustrated by the Canopus of Hadrian's Villa.

During the Italian Renaissance a new harmony of conception and execution elevated garden statuary to an art form of rare quality. The gods, heroes and other figures from ancient mythology continued to provide the majority of subjects; in fact quantities of statues, such as those removed from Hadrian's Villa to the Villa d'Este, were plundered from ancient sites and repositioned in the gardens of acquisitive Renaissance patrons in order to recreate scenes of classical antiquity.

At the same time subjects were beginning to be chosen mainly to allow the artist to express his own genius; they offered a challenge to the questing minds of Renaissance craftsmen. The exquisite small bronze by Verrocchio, *Boy with a Dolphin*, is an ideal example. It was originally made to adorn a fountain in the garden of the Medici villa at Careggi. (It is now in the Palazzo Vecchio in Florence.) Verrocchio, a Renaissance artist of decisive importance who was a pupil of Donatello and himself taught Leonardo da Vinci, chose the delightful subject because it enabled him to express constant movement which varied as the statue was viewed from all angles. Thus garden statuary took a decisive step forward. No longer was it purely representational but a means of displaying different forms or groups in an environment.

Verrocchio's 'Boy with a Dolphin' was made for a fountain, and became widely influential in later garden sculpture.

*The dark gods of the soil are never entirely absent from even the most rational of gardens —
hence the continued appropriateness of pagan mythology. Nowhere is this feeling more
powerful than at Bomarzo, north of Rome, where between 1552 and 1580 Pier Francesco
Orsini laid out the most bizarre of all landscapes, carving the natural rocks into shapes of
humans, animals and monsters. This giant represents the Appenines. Right: Jan Van
Nost's lead figure of Pan at Rousham, Oxfordshire.*

The dramatic strength of Scheemakers' *Lion Attacking a Horse* at Rousham is quite different from the arcadian quality which William Kent achieved in the rest of the garden and which is exemplified by the choice and position of statues in and around the Vale of Venus, all of which are ideally suited to the natural wooded setting. Venus herself, shown on page 108, stands upon one of the cascades in the valley and below her Pan and other characters blend in with their leafy surroundings. The figures were all made by Jan van Nost in lead, of which Gertrude Jekyll was later to pronounce herself a firm advocate: 'There can scarcely be a doubt that the happiest material for our garden sculpture and ornament is lead.'

The work of Van Nost, who came from Flanders to England at the end of the 17th century, had an important influence upon the widespread use of lead which, from a practical point of view had shown itself to be a preferable material for statuary in English gardens because of its ability to withstand damp and rain better than most stonework. The warmth of its texture and the manner in which it weathers with age, was particularly admired, especially when compared to more ornate but coldly formal material such as marble.

Prior to his work for Rousham, Van Nost had worked at Melbourne Hall, where he established his reputation and for which he supplied his most important single piece, the Four Seasons urn, which marked his highest achievement in decorative leadwork. The lead figures he made for the garden included a number of pairs of winged *amorini* or *putti*, statues of Perseus and Andromeda and the lead figure of Mercury shown on page 109, suitably elevated on an impressive pedestal in the centre of the main sweep of garden which runs from the house down to the formal basin and Robert Bakewell's Birdcage Arbour. A number of other important pieces of lead statuary in different gardens have been attributed to Van Nost. Some of the most delightful are the group of rustic figures who stand on the balustrade of one of the terraces at Powis Castle.

Lead figures representing a romantic picture of rural life, such as the ones at Powis, were ideally suitable in England during the 18th century and variations upon this theme were produced for numerous gardens. John Cheere, one of Van

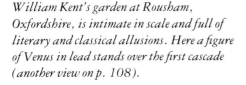

William Kent's garden at Rousham, Oxfordshire, is intimate in scale and full of literary and classical allusions. Here a figure of Venus in lead stands over the first cascade (another view on p. 108).

Lead figure of the god Mercury at Buscot Park, Oxfordshire, the garden laid out by Harold Peto, c.1904-11: a perfect use of statuary in association with water.

Nost's most distinguished successors, made the pair at Charlecote Park in Warwickshire, one of which is shown on page 113. In some of his other work Cheere demonstrated how successfully leadwork could be painted, notably in the Nymph of the Grot he made for Stourhead, and painted figures such as the shepherdess at Antony House on page 112 added an element of colourful vitality to statuary of the period.

One important characteristic of leadwork was that, being made from moulds, it could be liberally reproduced; in this it heralded the techniques which were to spread to other materials during the 19th century and have an important influence upon both statuary and other ornament in English gardens. As the Victorians increasingly looked to the past for inspiration for their garden styles and models for their statuary and other decoration, so it became easier to reproduce these models. This as much as anything else was responsible for the repetitive nature of much ornamental gardening during the Victorian era.

***Pagan deities** still preside over the cycle of nature. Above left: Diana and (in the distance) Hercules at St Paul's Walden Bury, Hertfordshire. Above right: Neptune at Würzburg, Bavaria; and Venus, a lead copy of the Borghese Venus, at Rousham. Right: Mercury, another version of Giambologna's famous statue, at Melbourne, Derbyshire, with Robert Bakewell's wrought-iron 'Birdcage' arbour, seen in detail on p.68, behind.*

There was nothing either eccentric or surprising about the collections of statuary made to fill the French gardens of the 17th century. At Versailles their production and display reached a level that is unrivalled both in quality and quantity. Their subject matter is largely Italian, but they are deployed by the French with military precision, vital elements in the desired picture of ordered harmony.

In the gardens designed by André le Nôtre each statue had its own carefully planned position in the overall scheme – conveying a meaning that was both visual and allegorical. In great numbers they represented a suitably noble decorative style, while the vertical proportions of their forms, whether silhouetted against open sky or set against a background of clipped hedge or trees, perfectly complemented the broad horizontal sweeps of parterre and water.

In their collaboration at Vaux-le-Vicomte Le Nôtre and Charles Le Brun, who organized the sculpture programme for the garden, first demonstrated their ability to create a scene of unprecedented majesty. The positioning of the statues on lofty pedestals emphasized the flawless logic of the design while the figures they portrayed – such as Diana the huntress – elevated the spirit of the garden to the level of the gods of the ancient world. At the same time the demand for such quantities of statuary led to a quality of workmanship which rivalled that of the Italian Renaissance.

After the disgrace of Fouquet many of the statues were removed from the garden at Vaux-le-Vicomte by Louis XIV and taken to one of the many royal gardens. Meanwhile at Versailles the steady flow of commissions for different parts of the garden was producing the greatest collection of statuary ever created. Nothing was left to chance: plaster models were even put out on rough wooden pedestals in their intended positions to ensure they were the right size. Le Brun himself conceived the various groups and their intended position within the gardens as well as drawing out the initial designs to which his team of sculptors subsequently worked.

Versailles: the Bassin de Latone. Latona, one of the loves of Jupiter, was Apollo's mother, which accounts for her central position in the garden. She was persecuted by Juno and forced to wander the world as a fugitive. In Caria she was insulted by peasants, whom Jupiter punished by turning them into frogs. They are seen here inhabiting the three rings of the fountain, two or three of them actually in process of transformation.

Venus, one of the innumerable classical figures at Versailles. The allegorical programme worked out by Le Brun must always have been an effort to follow; now that so many statues have been moved, it is even more so. But their enchanting visual effect remains.

Many of the statues were copies of famous ancient figures, such as Venus, and Laocöon and his two sons. Others were subjects chosen by Le Brun to play their part in the grand allegory which dominated the whole scheme. The allegory revolved around the representation of Louis XIV as the Sun in the figure of Apollo. It encompassed scenes from Apollo's myth and was further developed in a series of themes. Reclining figures representing the great rivers of France were positioned in the Water Parterre while elsewhere were groups representing the seasons, the times of the day, the elements, the muses and the four quarters of the globe. The virtuosity of subject matter was matched by the richness of materials used: stone, marble, bronze and gilded lead.

The sculpture programme for Versailles and its successful introduction to the gardens was a plan of staggering complexity and ambition, only made possible by the combined genius and vision of Le Nôtre and Le Brun – as well as the millions of French *livres* which it cost Louis XIV. Its intrinsic importance is demonstrated by imagining the great allées and vistas without the rows of statues for they are the visible and tangible confirmation of the statement which Louis XIV made in his gardens, as well as being ornamental decoration of unsurpassed quality.

Shepherds and shepherdesses have always seemed suitable inhabitants of gardens. The charming shepherdess (left) of painted plaster is at Antony House, in Cornwall; the lead shepherd (above), attributed to Henry Cheere, at Charlecote, Warwickshire. Right: flower-child, Victorian style, at Knightshayes, Devon.

Initially statues were made for fountains or for prominent positions within the garden. As the Renaissance moved into the Baroque, however, the treatment became more flamboyant; figures were incorporated into the architecture of gardens or displayed in the most theatrical manner posssible. At the Villa Garzoni the staircases linking the three main terraces terminate at the top in two massive pillars against which satyrs — one of which is shown on page 129 — recline, resting the hooves of their goat-like legs against scrolls of stonework. Above, the top of the cascade is flanked by two majestic figures representing the cities of Florence and Lucca, who gaze out across the descending levels of garden to the countryside beyond. And nothing could be more theatrical than the garden's upper climax, the figure of Fame blowing a great jet of water from her trumpet into the pool below.

One of the monstrous faces in the Orsini garden at Bomarzo — the entrance to a cave, for those who dare to go in.

The figure of Florence with her emblem the lion looks out over the garden of the Villa Garzoni. Statuary is vital in giving content and atmosphere to a garden, often defining and making explicit the designer's attitude to man and nature.

Allegorical statues on a monumental scale appeared in a number of Italian gardens, such as Bartolommeo Ammanati's figure of the Apennines at the Medici Villa at Castello, but at one garden, the Villa Orsini at Bomarzo, the idea was taken to extraordinary – at times disturbing – limits. The garden was made by Pierfrancesco Orsini between 1550 and 1570 and went against all the accepted tenets of Renaissance design. It was neither formal nor architectural and only its bizarre subject matter and inspiration from the *sacro bosco* of ancient literature would have appealed to the imaginative Renaissance mind.

In the mysterious wooded setting which Orsini created, large natural outcrops of rock were carved into a series of enormous sculptures. In one place is a recumbent giant shown on page 104, and in another is carved a huge face whose open mouth has a span which enables a man easily to stand in it and forms the entrance to a cave. These and the other monstrous figures in the garden – a dragon attacking lions, a huge tortoise and a giant tearing the legs of a victim apart– all have a nightmarish quality not found in any other Italian garden.

No subsequent garden has ever boasted sculptures quite on the scale of the Villa Orsini but animals, birds and other creatures of more modest proportions have often been portrayed in gardens of different periods throughout Europe, as illustrated by the selection of pictures on pages 116 and 117. Dogs, such as the one in Harold Peto's garden at Iford Manor, shown on page 117, have been frequently used to represent guardians or sentinels, while the monkeys at the Villa Garzoni and the German Rococo garden at Veitshochheim introduce an element of humour.

The pair of cranes on page 116 belong to the garden of Whatton in Leicestershire, made towards the end of the 19th century, which boasts a most eccentric collection of statuary. They are the most normal of a series of bronze Chinese figures, whose bizarre and unexpected appearances create an element of surprise which harks back to the spirit of the Villa Orsini.

Animals and birds are a garden's natural residents and often have particular significance in sculptural form. This pair of cranes in the Chinese garden at Whatton House, Leicestershire, represent long life. The dog who sits as guardian at Iford Manor, Wiltshire (above right), was bought by the architect in Italy. Below right: two denizens of Baroque gardens, at the Villa Garzoni, Tuscany, and Veitshochheim in Bavaria.

One of the most ambitious of all Rococo statuary groups is Ferdinand Tietze's centrepiece at Veitshochheim, in Bavaria, of 1702. On a base representing Parnassus, surrounded by figures of the muses, the winged horse Pegasus is about to leap up to Olympus.

Nothing like Versailles was ever created again but it became the supreme model for gardens throughout Europe for over a century. In France this influence combined with an instinctive desire to see a balance of order and decoration to ensure that statuary continued to be of primary importance. Elsewhere in Europe the reputation of Versailles was virtually unquestioned, while the French style was spread abroad by a number of French architects and garden designers. One of Le Nôtre's most able pupils, Charles Le Blond, was employed by Peter the Great as the senior architect in St Petersburg. Although he only lived in Russia for three years before his premature death in 1719 he was the decisive figure in the creation of the gardens of Peterhof.

The French influence was probably most widespread in Germany where, during the second half of the 17th century and the 18th century, numerous gardens were created in which statuary was usually the major form of decoration. During the 18th century, as the grandeur of Baroque which called for a dominant overall layout, softened into the more light-hearted Rococo, the details of individual ornaments were no longer restricted by their place in the master-plan – as shown best in the Hofgarten of Veitshochheim in Bavaria, created during the 1760s.

No longer is the garden's shape and position controlled by its relationship with the schloss. Instead the design of the garden, which is divided up by hedges, incorporates regular surprises which would have been unthinkable during the stately Baroque era. Along all of the hedged walks and in the series of enclosed garden rooms stand the numerous statues which give the garden its character and are among the best expressions of Rococo decorative art.

While many of the three hundred statues have conventional subjects such as various gods, the arts and the seasons, the great difference is in their treatment which is no longer serene and impressively classical, but frivolous and fanciful, and the chief aim was to delight and amuse rather than impress. The statues were largely the work of Ferdinand Dietz (or Tietz) who showed himself to be the most imaginative and accomplished German sculptor of the period.

Almost contemporary with Veitshochheim was the creation of the garden at Château Canon which similarly reveals a development away from rigid formality. Here the influence is English for Elie de Beaumont, who made the garden, numbered Horace Walpole among his friends and had certainly visited Stowe when in England. The main design of the garden is axial within a woodland setting. From the château grass slopes to an ornamental lake beyond which a broad avenue rises away. Around the lake Beaumont arranged a series of classical statues and busts in a seemingly arbitrary manner whose effect relied far more upon their setting than their interrelationship. It reflected the positioning of ornament in a natural – if somewhat idealized – setting which Beaumont would have witnessed at Stowe and which was best expressed in English gardens during the first half of the 18th century.

The garden of Château Canon, in Normandy, owes much to English influence. Here a series of classical busts on pedestals make an effective formal grouping (see overleaf). The effect is one of an idyllic natural landscape, filled with beautiful and harmonious presences.

Figure sculpture, often only vaguely identified or not identified at all, serves as a focus to
a layout or as a means of directing the eye. Opposite top: cloaked male figures in the
18th-century Rococo garden at Veitshochheim and at Torosay, the latter also 18th century
and Venetian. Left: a charming Victorian lead female figure at Athelhampton. At Canon,
Normandy (above), the stone nymph stands at the centre of a group of classical busts.

The most Italianate of English gardens is that of Renishaw Hall, Derbyshire, where Sir George Sitwell placed a series of overlifesize statues in a formal sequence from the house to the open country.

The most important single influence upon Victorian garden design came from Italy and the creations of the Renaissance. Sweeping terraces, lavish parterres and fountains, and the decoration of gardens with statues of Roman gods and heroes were widely admired. In some cases the results were startling and bore little resemblance to the original model but in other instances gardens were made which represented a skilful adaptation of the Italian ideal to English conditions.

One of the most restrained and successful examples was the Emperor's Walk laid out at Grimston Park in Yorkshire by William Nesfield, where busts of the twelve Caesars stood on either side of the broad path leading to a porticoed temple. Nesfield's creation no longer exists (the sculpture was sold in the 1920s) but a comparable example is the Caesar's Lawn at Madresfield Court in Worcestershire, laid out during the 1870s, where busts of the twelve emperors are set in niches in a long yew hedge.

The 6th Earl Beauchamp, who added the Caesar's Lawn at Madresfield, was not content with reproduced statuary made for him in England and went to Italy himself to choose and collect his set of busts. A number of other Englishmen did the same, especially around the turn of the century, when gardens had shed much of their Victorian opulence, and a number of outstanding architectural Italian gardens were created.

Arguably the most successful was that at Renishaw Hall in Derbyshire, made by the eccentric Sir George Sitwell who was both passionate and knowledgeable about Italian Renaissance gardens, gaining his information during frequent stays at his castle of Montegufoni outside Florence. At Renishaw the gardens are designed in a series of irregular terraces leading from the romantic façade of the house to where the parkland drops away. At the bottom of the impressive slope Sir George dug a lake to complete the picture. The ornamental highlights of the garden are the three superb pairs of statues which Sir George brought from Italy and which occupy key positions in the garden. On either side of the point where the central axis descends the steps of the main terrace are Neptune and Diana who, like the pair of giants beyond them flanking the steps at the garden's edge, look outward to the surrounding countryside. Although the statues are few in number they are completely responsible for the Italian character of the garden.

Perhaps not surprisingly, it was in Italy, at the Villa La Pietra in Florence, that the most admired recreation of an Italian garden was made by an Englishman. The 17th-century villa and remnants of its contemporary garden were owned by Arthur Acton who began work on his garden in 1904. The sloping site was made into three terraces each with its own cross-axis leading to circular areas enclosed by clipped hedges. Throughout the garden Acton arranged a wonderful collection of Venetian statuary and it is these figures and their positions which elevate the garden both visually and atmospherically. Statues stand along the balustrade of the first terrace, as is shown on page 160, and at all focal points and junctions in the garden. The most strongly Renaissance feature is the green theatre recalling the spirit of gardens such as the Villa Marlia near Lucca.

Arthur Acton's ingenious green theatre at La Pietra, Florence: statues and balustrades for scenery, yew hedges for wings. The footlights are concealed in the box globes.

Art and nature unite to give subtle meaning to the garden architect's concept. At the
Palazzo Farnese, Caprarola, of 1556-78, overlifesize caryatids line the perimeter wall,
reflecting the visitor's attention back into the garden. At Godinton Park, Kent (opposite),
Reginald Blomfield used the Italianate idea of columnar screens and classical statues but
gave them a setting of English planting.

Gardens such as Renishaw and La Pietra emphasize the importance not only of the subject matter of statuary but of their position within the garden. During most of the 20th century opportunities for formal gardens on such a scale have been few, but in many cases the Italian influence has remained. At Tyninghame in Scotland, illustrated on page 128, the sweeping vista with its harmony of yew hedges, statues brought from Vicenza and rolling hills in the distance, is highly theatrical and would certainly have appealed to the garden makers of the Italian Renaissance.

The influence of Italy and classical figures have been of primary importance in the evolution of garden statuary and largely account for the quantity of reproduction work since the beginning of the Victorian era. During the 20th century in particular, however, gardens have tended to be on a far smaller scale than previously and the atmosphere is more intimate and domestic. This is reflected in the statuary chosen, such as the girl with a flower-basket at Knightshayes in Devon and the similar stone child at Arbigland in Scotland.

The most important development to affect statuary during the 20th century has been the emergence of modern abstract and non-figurative sculpture. As will be discussed in a later section, possibly because of the deeply entrenched nature of English gardening traditions, modern sculpture has not been so popular in English gardens as in many other countries, notably the United States. As a result its appearance in private gardens has been limited and figurative sculpture, whether in a contemporary or classical style, remains more widely accepted.

La Pietra, Florence: two statues more romantic than classical – a young woman holding a baby and a warrior with sword and shield.

A child with a basket of fruit at Arbigland, in Scotland, sadly contemplates the fallen leaves, as if surprised that summer is over.

At Tyninghame, *East Lothian, the central allée of the walled garden, laid out this century, is flanked by sets of statues from Vicenza representing Music and the Seasons. The design itself, with a formal vista opening into the surrounding landscape, is also strongly Italianate. Above: the end of a balustrade at the Villa Garzoni, where a satyr leans against a richly carved pillar, is part of the grand staircase.*

129

Urns and vases

Together with statuary, urns and vases have been throughout history the most important free-standing garden ornament. Some of the grandest and most harmonious effects have been achieved when the two have been used together, as at Versailles where rows of alternating marble statues and urns march down either side of the *Tapis Vert* between the Bassin de Latone and the Bassin d'Apollon.

At the same time no other type of ornament has so successfully combined a decorative role with a practical one, or had its basic form adapted to so many different styles and materials. As a result there is no garden for which some sort of urn is not suitable, from the most impressive formal layouts of the past to the smallest urban garden of this century, where limited planting space makes such decorative containers invaluable.

The aesthetic attraction of the urn, both to the artists and craftsmen who have made them and to the eye of the more ordinary beholder, has been that it is supremely adaptable to all proportions and to all manner of decoration without ever losing the perfect symmetry of its circular shape. This adaptability has meant that in terms of garden ornament its uses have been legion. When made to alternate with statues it completes the reciprocal harmony between animate and inanimate beauty; architecturally its shape and outline complement the geometric lines of terrace walls, balustrades, or gate piers; while its shape and texture are the perfect foil to either clipped hedges or to any plants it may contain.

Since the earliest civilizations the ashes of the dead have been placed in urns and this connection has invested them with a strong mystique. At times such as the 18th century in England they have been regarded as deeply symbolic, and in addition of enormous architectural significance because of their importance in the classical tradition.

Thousands of years ago the Egyptians first used simple earthenware vases in their gardens. The vases contained small trees and shrubs and were placed at the corners of rectangular beds or at the ends of paths. As well as having a pleasing appearance the vases served the practical function of retaining water for whatever was planted in them – something that was always difficult in such a hot climate. From this simple beginning urns and vases have gone through ceaseless elaboration and yet this most fundamental use as a decorative container has continued until the present day.

We owe to the Greeks the discovery that plants can be effectively 'forced' – made to grow more quickly than is natural – by being grown in pots. As a result they die off more quickly after flowering. Such plants were grown for the annual festival of Adonis when their rapid withering symbolized his early death. The Romans built upon the traditions of both the Egyptians and the Greeks but it was not until the Italian Renaissance that the urn began to be used extensively for both practical and decorative purposes.

Not often do urns manage to convey a sinister quality, but these, looming through the mist at Bomarzo, are strangely in keeping with the prevailing atmosphere of menace. In the background a stone dragon tears at its prey.

The chaste shape of the classical urn went through an amazing series of transformations during the Baroque era. Kent's urn at Rousham (below), one of a pair in front of the seven-arched Praeneste, is still austerely Roman. But the French urns used at Birr Castle, Co. Offaly, Ireland (left), have become exercises in Rococo imagination that takes them into a different world.

In the earliest Renaissance gardens such as the Medici villa at Careggi terracotta urns containing orange and lemon trees were important features of formally planned flower gardens. They became one of the most familiar features of Italian gardens and were used almost universally. Initially the urns — or pots, for they were essentially humble and practical containers — were undecorated and even later were usually only ever adorned with simple swags. Smaller pots contained scented flowers and herbs.

Quite different were the urns and vases which appeared along the balustrades of terraces, around fountains, on gate piers and screens — in fact throughout the gardens as a regular feature of architectural ornament. The function of these ornamental urns is essentially architectural and it is with their appearance that the range of designs and decorative styles suddenly expands dramatically. In some of the most lavish gardens there might be between ten and twenty different styles of urn, arranged in pairs if not larger groups, varying from the plainest of Greek-inspired *amphorae* to richly carved and fluted specimens complete with decorated bases and lids.

Italian urns and vases were almost exclusively made of stone or terracotta so as to blend most satisfactorily with the architectural features they usually adorned. This was also the case in most formal French gardens, where ornamental urns and vases were being used extensively by the end of the 16th century and at the Château

The château of Valençay, Indre, is a 16th-century building added to in the 18th century, when the present garden was designed. Its use of urns and statuary is conventional enough, but the urns themselves (right) are among the most elaborate and imaginative of their time.

de Brécy in Normandy their sculptured decoration was brought to an extraordinary peak of Mannerist ingenuity, as shown on page 141. The garden was laid out around the middle of the 17th century in a series of five terraces ascending from the relatively modest château. Flights of central steps link the terraces and on the fourth terrace the steps are flanked by monumental gate piers. The fifth terrace is deliberately narrow and steps lead to similar piers on the edge of the garden with wrought iron gates. Throughout the garden the retaining walls of the terraces or balustrading, the enclosing side walls and the gate piers are surmounted with wonderfully carved vases or, in some places, stone finials incorporating three mythical eagles. Many of the vases stand upon scrolled feet and their slender tops support arrangements of fruit and flowers, while those upon the gate piers add a heroic element to their appearance.

In the later garden of the Château de Valençay the arrangement of majestic vases alternating with statues is heroic in a quite different manner and is reminiscent of the *tapis vert* at Versailles. At Valençay the château, begun during the 16th century and expanded at intervals during the next two hundred years, is far larger and more imposing than Brécy and this is reflected in the size and position of the vases and other garden ornaments. Together Brécy and Valençay illustrate the decorative versatility of vases and urns and the degrees to which it was utilized in the French formal garden.

Urns holding flowers are among the most versatile of garden ornaments. Opposite top: at Versailles at the end of a terrace; and at Herriard Park, Hampshire. Left: the formal layout at the Château de Sassy, Normandy. Above: Bramham Park, Yorkshire, an early 18th-century garden close to the style of Le Nôtre. The Broad Walk is terminated by an obelisk at one end and an Ionic Temple at the other.

Where the French influence was strongest in English gardens, similarly impressive urns were placed in prominent positions, as in the Great Fountain Garden at Hampton Court. But by the end of the 17th century radical innovations in English garden design were being matched by increasingly original and brilliant craftsmanship. This is exemplified in two particular urns, one made for Melbourne Hall in Derbyshire, the other for Bramham Park in Yorkshire. The Four Seasons urn at Melbourne by Van Nost is a piece of leadwork of unique virtuosity. Its stone counterpart at Bramham, also depicting the seasons but called the Four Faces urn, is hardly less impressive. Both stand at junctions of formal *allées* showing a different face in every direction.

Urns can play key roles in the design of a formal garden. Below: the Great Fountain Garden at Hampton Court.

Two especially fine urns. Below: the lead Four Seasons urn at Melbourne, Derbyshire, by Jan van Nost. Right: the Four Faces urn at Bramham, Yorkshire, in stone, which in fact also depicts the seasons.

During the 18th century in England the urn became an object of universal admiration, even reverence. The architectural qualities of its shape, which satisfied the Palladian requirement for putting proportion and balance before decoration, united with its capacity to recall the classical perfection of the ancient world and the values that it evoked: solemnity, chastity and harmony. William Kent certainly had these qualities in mind when he designed the Praeneste terrace at Rousham with urns, one of which is shown on page 133, at either end. Early in the next century similar feelings were expressed by John Keats in the *Ode on a Grecian Urn*:

> *'Thou still unravish'd bride of quietness,*
> *Thou foster-child of Silence and slow Time,*
> *Sylvan historian who canst thus express*
> *A flowery tale more sweetly than our rhyme:*
> *What leaf-fringed legend haunts about thy shape*
> *Of deities or mortals or of both,*
> *In Tempe or the dales of Arcady?'*

One of the most ardent supporters of the urn as a form of garden ornament was William Shenstone, the poet and landscape gardener who was influential in the development of the Picturesque Movement. Both Shenstone's extensive correspondence and his volume *Unconnected Thoughts on Gardening* are filled with references to the quality of urns, in particular when used as memorials. His own garden contained many, all inscribed with a dedication, as did those of the friends and acquaintances whom he advised.

No self-respecting devotee of the Picturesque would have contemplated actually planting anything in an urn: their use was ornamental and symbolic. The return of flower gardening and its rapid expansion during the Victorian era prompted quite different views and in attempts to recreate scenes of Italian and French formality flower parterres were liberally decorated with urns and vases. Some were purely ornamental but others were filled with the brightly coloured annuals which were raised by the thousand in hot-houses and conservatories. Once again urns and vases were as important for practical purposes as they were for ornamental ones and this has been the case ever since.

The unobtrusive urn *punctuates the line of a balustrade or marks a turning line, often suggesting flowers by its shape if it does not actually contain them. Above, top left to bottom right: the Villa Lante, Bagnaia; Bramham Park, Yorkshire; Athelhampton, Dorset; and Powis Castle, Wales. Opposite: a particularly splendid example, matching the richness of the parterre below, at the Château de Brécy, Normandy, 17th century, restored.*

The 19th century saw a rapid expansion of the suburban middle classes who enjoyed gardens and desired to own them. At the same time improvements in cast iron and artificial stone meant that almost anything could be cheaply reproduced, so they were able to afford the ornamental urns and vases which were such popular features. Classical, Renaissance or French Baroque styles would all be turned out in limitless quantities and thus most garden ornaments were no longer the exclusive privilege of the rich.

Even so, it was the rich and the owners of large houses who created the most spectacular effects. In the fashionable Italian-style gardens created by William Nesfield and Charles Barry, urns and vases were the most important free-standing ornaments. Look, for instance, at the parterres they laid out in gardens such as

Nymans, Sussex: here a Byzantine basin forms a strong centrepiece to the Sunken Garden. The Italianate loggia behind (also shown on p.44) keeps up the Mediterranean mood.

Anglesey Abbey, Cambridgeshire, is rich in monumental urns. This unusual one of porphyry is given its own miniature temple with a copper roof.

Trentham in Staffordshire, Harewood House in Yorkshire and Cliveden in Buckinghamshire, or at Barry's treatment of the great staircase at Shrublands Park in Suffolk, his most dramatic essay in the Italian manner.

By the end of the 19th century the desire for ornamental containers for plants led gardeners to look beyond the traditionally used urns and pots to other objects which could be used or re-used in attractive ways. Lead cisterns and water butts, many of them with delicately worked decoration perhaps incorporating coats of arms, came into favour, many of them bearing dates from the 17th and 18th centuries when they were originally made to hold water. So did large coppers and sarcophagi, which could often be found with highly detailed reliefs. The originals in stone or marble were expensive, but they could be reproduced in cheaper materials.

Urns and the sort of similar containers mentioned above are easily transportable and most of those that can be seen in gardens today have moved a number of times since they were originally made. For collectors of antique ornament they have often proved the most attractive and obtainable items, filling prominent positions in English gardens. At Nymans in Sussex the great Byzantine urn which was brought to the garden by Leonard Messel between the wars stands in the centre of the Sunken Garden, creating an image of great architectural strength when viewed with the Italian loggia in the background.

One of the most avid collectors of the century was Huttleston Broughton, 1st Lord Fairhaven, who began creating the classical landscape around Anglesey Abbey, Cambridgeshire, shortly after he bought the house in 1926. The enormous garden is planned around the various urns, statues and other ornaments which he steadily collected, all of them antique or original works of the highest quality. They include a pair of bronze urns which came from the Bagatelle garden in Paris and a monumental pair of French urns from Stafford House in London. The most unusual is the porphyry urn which was placed within its own temple of Doric columns and copper roof.

143

Flowers may be allowed to overflow their containers with picturesque effect. This composition at the Villa Garzoni is made up of several pots and urns so that plants cascade from every level. At Torosay Castle, Isle of Mull (opposite above), a copper urn planted with conifers marks the crossing of two axes. Right: almost everything can hold flowers — a lead trough at the Villa Reale, Castello; and a classical sarcophagus at Blenheim Palace, Oxfordshire.

Filling an urn with flowers softens its outline and brings it closer to nature. Here, at Buscot Park, Oxfordshire, two overflowing urns give ceremonial dignity to the top of a staircase.

Opposite: a flowering urn used as the centrepiece of a vista at Renishaw, Derbyshire.

Harold Peto's garden at Iford Manor is one of the most striking examples of a garden being created to display a most varied collection of garden ornament, gathered from different countries and originating from different periods. As well as the statuary which ranges from human figures to deer, dogs and birds, and innumerable different styles of urn and vase, there are many other antique architectural features such as the well-head shown on page 148. At Buscot Park in Oxfordshire, where he was not working for himself, Peto was more restrained in the quantity of ornament with which he decorated the garden, but the same eye for quality is clearly evident, for instance in the pair of urns which he positioned at one corner of the house and the obelisks at the entrance to one of the avenues shown on page 149.

Peto's example was followed by many of his contemporaries such as Sir George Sitwell who positioned a pair of Veronese marble fountains as the centrepieces of two of the formal yew-hedged enclosures in his garden at Renishaw. Collections as large as Peto's have rarely been assembled during the subsequent decades of this century, but the variety of objects re-used as free-standing ornament has, if anything, expanded. At Arley Hall in Cheshire a stone finial which once surmounted a wall or balustrade provides an architectural balance to the planting in one part of the garden, while at Meadowbrook Farm in Pennsylvania the combination of the modern sundial with an antique capital at its base demonstrates the imagination and ingenuity which have regularly been shown in the re-use of free-standing ornaments.

Sundials, capitals, obelisks . . . *a huge variety of objects, mostly associated with some function even if no longer fulfilling it, constitute incidents in the garden space. Left: a sundial at Heaselands, Sussex; a finial at Arley Hall, Cheshire; a modern sundial on an antique capital at Meadowbrook Farm, Pennsylvania; and a classical well-head re-used at Iford Manor, Wiltshire. Above: antique obelisks flanking one of Peto's three axes at Buscot Park, Oxfordshire.*

The Hofgarten at Veitshochheim, Bavaria, is divided into small spaces by tall hedges and furnished as a series of outdoor rooms, a combination of treillage and fanciful wooden seats.

Furniture

The veneration which the 18th-century poet and gardener William Shenstone felt towards urns and their place in the garden was only marginally stronger than his similar feelings towards garden seats. In the garden or 'landskip' which he created at his home The Leasowes near Birmingham there were no less than thirty-nine seats within the relatively limited area of some thirty acres. Each seat was positioned so as to ensure that the visitor should enjoy a particular view or prospect, and suitable feelings of repose or excitement were encouraged by the mottoes or poems with which each was adorned. On one the visitor was greeted with the words:

> *'And tread with awe these favour'd bowers,*
> *Nor wound the shrub nor bruise the flowers;*
> *So may your path with sweets abound!*
> *So may your couch with rest be crown'd!*
> *But harm betide the wayward swain,*
> *Who dares our hallow'd haunts profane.'*

Few people have valued garden seats quite so highly as Shenstone, but many would agree in seeing them as places of rest from which a view of a garden or a more expansive prospect may be enjoyed. Seats have been incorporated into garden architecture for centuries. Tables, on the other hand, are essentially a recent feature, brought into the garden by the desire to use it as an extension of the house.

People disagree about whether garden seats should be treated as pieces of garden ornament in their own right and therefore be decorative and striking, or whether they should be as unobtrusive as possible. Gertrude Jekyll held characteristically robust views on the subject: 'The common habit of painting garden seats a dead white is certainly open to criticism. The seat should not be made too conspicuous. Like all other painted things about a garden: gates, railings, or flower-tubs, the painting should be such as to suit the environment; it should in no case be so glaring as to draw almost exclusive attention to itself.'

Considering her strong opinions, it is unthinkable that the original seats designed by Edwin Lutyens for a number of gardens in which they collaborated would have been painted white, as has been done almost universally with subsequent reproductions of them, such as the one at Montacute. Here the seat is positioned as a prominent focal point along one of the garden's main axes, providing the foreground of the view out from the raised walk along the edge of the garden to the countryside beyond and looking back across the fountain pool in the centre of the formal sunken garden towards the house.

In total contrast is the position of the simple stone bench at Vaux-le-Vicomte shown on page 156, whose functional simplicity would no doubt have appealed to Miss Jekyll. Situated in the garden's main parterre beyond the house, the bench blends into the overall design without playing an active role and in no way intrudes into the grand vista. In both French Baroque gardens such as Vaux-le-Vicomte and Italian Renaissance ones, seats were only treated in an ornamental and architectural manner where they occupied a position of axial importance as at the end of a vista or against a boundary wall, or did not intrude into the planning of a parterre. In such cases they were often given highly decorated arms and feet, as illustrated by the terracotta seat at the Villa Garzoni.

One of the Villa Garzoni's fantastic chairs, modelled on examples from ancient Rome with an oriental flavour. The arms are winged lions whose wings meet behind to form the back.

Places of repose are selected at points where the garden repays contemplation, and the furniture must be part of the mood. At Carnell, in Scotland (below), an oriental atmosphere is evoked by the Chinese Chippendale seat, the lantern and the attendant dragons. Earlshall Castle, Fife (opposite), was laid out by Robert Lorimer only this century; the seat in a covered arbour closes one of the vistas.

A well placed seat on the terrace at Montacute provides the logical climax of the view, and at the same time suggests the idea of lingering to look back in the opposite direction: one of the ways in which the garden designer can manipulate the spectator's experience.

The principle that garden seats should blend into the general appearance of a garden has been maintained by designers and architects of all periods. At Godinton Park Reginald Blomfield designed and positioned the curving stone seat shown on page 157 ideally. It repeats the shape of the balustraded belvedere behind, while its simple construction with no back enables the sitter to enjoy either the view out across the belvedere to the park beyond or the one in the opposite direction across the formal lily pool into the garden.

A seat situated as the focal point of a vista should beckon at the same time. It provides a reward when one finally arrives at it. This quality is captured at Earlshall in Scotland in the plan by Sir Robert Lorimer illustrated on page 153. A path leads between yew topiary to the almost circular wooden seat set in an arched niche. Together they create an arresting scene to be approached and equally satisfying views out. Lorimer was a craftsman to whom such details as the correct design of a seat were as important as they were to his 18th-century predecessor, William Kent. At Rousham Kent designed a delightful pair of small pedimented, trellis-work pavilions incorporating seats, one of which is illustrated on page 73. Quite different, and on a suitably grand scale, was his design of a far larger stone classical temple at Holkham Hall in Norfolk, which had open arcades on all four sides but incorporated a seat facing in the direction from which the temple was approached.

Kent's pavilion seats at Rousham heralded the fashion for trellis-work designs which combined with the Chinese influence during the mid-18th century to produce some of the most elaborate geometric designs for wooden seats. Today these are among the most popular objects of reproduction and loosely referred to as being 'Chinese Chippendale', although Chippendale was by no means responsible for all of the designs to which the description is applied.

The Victorians enjoyed being inventive as much as they enjoyed being comfortable and both characteristics are confirmed in the myriad different styles of garden furniture which appeared during the 19th century. Wooden seats became especially popular later in the century when the Arts and Crafts Movement popularized rustic features, such as thatched summer-houses incorporating roughly worked seats, or innumerable variations on the circular wooden 'tree seat'. Most ingenious were wooden seats incorporating handles at one end and a wheel at the other, in the style of a wheelbarrow, which could be moved with ease from one site to another. These reflected a new development regarding the positioning of seats. Whereas in the 18th century and earlier seats were planned as part of the overall design and therefore permanent fixtures, it was now quite acceptable for them to be moved from one part of the garden to another.

Not so easily moveable were the cast-iron seats which were embellished with the richest designs, including backs of leaf-work or vines, arms which ended in the heads of animals or birds — harking back to the design of some Renaissance furniture— and occasionally legs also clothed in foliage.

The idea that the garden is a place of relaxation as much as a place of enjoyment and fulfillment has continued into the present century, so that today our gardens — or parts of them — are often described as 'outdoor rooms'. In this context furniture has become a feature of great importance; it is an area where new styles have appeared constantly at the same time as the most established older ones have been reproduced. The only danger of this desire for comfort in an era when virtually all gardens have to be constantly maintained is the temptation to forget Kipling's warning that

'gardens are not made
By singing, "Oh how beautiful!" and sitting in the shade'.

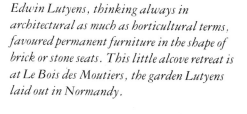

Edwin Lutyens, thinking always in architectural as much as horticultural terms, favoured permanent furniture in the shape of brick or stone seats. This little alcove retreat is at Le Bois des Moutiers, the garden Lutyens laid out in Normandy.

Plain stone seats at Vaux-le-Vicomte (left) are clearly meant to merge into the background, not to form part of the grand design. But at Godinton Park, Kent (top), by Reginald Blomfield, the seat cleverly echoes the shape of the balustraded belvedere behind. More fanciful benches occur at the 18th-century Fantaisie, Germany, and Leigh Hall Place, Kent, by George Devey.

*David Wynne's fountain of the 'Boy with a
Dolphin' at Pepsico, New York, has a certain
Rococo élan expressed in a modern idiom with
modern technology. The fountain can be seen in
its setting on p.185.*

III

THE MODERN GARDEN

DILEMMAS AND OPPORTUNITIES

Jamie Garnock

T HE SITING AND IMPACT of ornaments in the modern garden may have lost some of the glorious flamboyance that marks so much of their history, but their clarity and potency continue firmly undiminished. Gardens and their environments have become considerably more diverse, as have garden-owners and their aspirations. This, in turn, has had its effects on the style and setting of garden ornaments. Some of the repercussions are unavoidable; some simply pose difficulties; none of them puts the existence of such ornamentation in doubt. Ornaments remain as vital an ingredient in today's gardens as in any of the landscapes of past centuries.

In many countries, contemporary circumstances have certainly not erased an instinctive reverence for the traditional, however they may have curbed its excesses of grandeur. Serried ranks of gods ensconced in yew-lined avenues and temples to Diana on distant hills may no longer be so easily accommodated, but a multitude of more modest scenarios pay respectful homage to time-honoured principles.

This veneration in an age of fundamental change has not gone unopposed. Contemporary inspiration has responded with fresh symbolism and radical alternatives. Garden design itself has explored new concepts and statuary has evolved into ever more diverse materials and styles. Advances in technology alone can prompt novelties of design and presentation. Ornaments that involve water, for example, have historically attracted man's scientific prowess in the pursuit of the spectacular; with the advent of electricity and, more recently, computers and fibre optics, the choreography of water and light around statuary has increased in breadth. Special effects are as important now as they were in the 16th century when the fountains at the Villa d'Este, near Rome, were conceived.

Whatever the context of the garden, and whatever the approach of its owner, ornamentation of some sort rarely fails to play a part. From simple classical urns in stone to abstract sculptures in glass, polished stainless steel or wire-mesh, a wide range of requirements can be met. The versatility of garden ornaments has ensured their unfailing popularity and longevity.

The roles performed by ornaments in today's landscape are, in essence, little changed from their roles in earlier eras. They continue to serve those same aesthetic and practical needs that have been felt for as long as the composition of the view has exercised the mind. However radical the change in dimension or complexion of that view, the general balance and content of the picture it presents remain a constant challenge.

Focal points, subsidiary and incidental details, philosophical statements and personal whims – all can suggest a range of visual responses to draw the eye, from admiration and delight to provocation and disbelief.

Since time immemorial there have also been the mundane but unavoidable features of gardens that their owners have contrived to mask with touches of artistry. As smaller gardens have become more prevalent the importance of such artistry has increased. Walls, fences, trellis-work, gates, doorways, steps, furniture, summer-houses and sheds are more than ever likely to be prominent parts of the main picture. A touch, perhaps even only a hint, of elegance can transform the practical into the ornamental.

Classical inspiration has continued into the 20th century. At La Pietra, near Florence, during the early years of the century, Arthur Acton laid out the grounds of his 17th-century villa primarily to display his collection of antique sculpture. The overall picture is the best example of an Englishman's conception of a classical Italian garden. The villa and garden are now the home of his son, Sir Harold Acton.

The passage of time illustrates the inseparable link between the garden and ornamentation, a similarity of motive engendering a continuity of use. The ways in which both garden and garden-owner have changed have, however, threatened complications.

Historically, the garden very often enjoyed lavish dimensions and generous funding. Both its development as an art form and its unfolding pleasures were largely confined to those with means to provide them. A comparatively small number of people, either through ownership or patronage, created and fashioned the styles. Thus the substance and pattern of their ornaments inevitably reflected their own status and power. Classical lines, voluptuous curves and triumphant climaxes were transfused into comparable landscapes. The glorious symmetry between the inorganic and the organic produced a synergy that, in turn, promised spectacular results.

In the past this potential was realized with an ease of composition that is considerably less common today. Statuary could be commissioned to match the geography, architecture, politics and character of the moment. Craftsmen were available and affordable to satisfy exact requirements. The social and physical landscape inspired and became the raison d'être of its ornamentation. That ornamentation simply reflected a certain point in time. Establishing the same unity of design in today's cross currents is liable to involve a little more ingenuity.

The supreme heights of artistry achieved by such successful choreography of ornament and landscape created a legacy that has so far resisted radical change.

Populations have expanded, land has been subject to division and subdivision, wealth and expectations have become more widely spread. Gardening is now the pursuit of more people than ever before, most of whom are working in smaller dimensions and with more limited means than the garden owners of earlier eras. Still, however, they will tend to see the ground between the house and the outside world, whatever its size, as capable of expressing some sort of organization, pleasure and interest.

Well defined boundaries and their closer association with the house form a conscious and immediate stage on which to assemble characters and create atmosphere. A single ornament that might originally have been just one of the chorus line in a sweeping drama can be the main star of a smaller production. It can even be too prominent. Certainly the visual impact of the ornament in the more modest arena is immense, and intimacy places greater stress on scale, style and detail. If these qualities are at variance with the surroundings, careful handling will be needed to make the pleasures outweigh the problems.

The historical perspective

Translating historical truths into today's context is not necessarily easy. Harmonies can be established and the ornament's role and character be successfully co-ordinated with the site's ambience, even if they are potentially ill-matched. The siting of uncompromising classicism in a starkly contemporary setting, for instance, involves all sorts of difficulties which have to be faced for the scene to integrate as a whole. Sharp modernism can render such classical ornaments meaningful only if they are deliberately restyled to embody a longer perspective. Hence the success of the neo-classical ornament in contemporary surroundings.

Introducing modern art forms into traditional contexts is not always so problematic. Contemporary sculpture very often explores timeless themes, such as the essential spirit of mankind, the primeval forces of Nature, and their interrelationship, focusing especially on the purity and increasing vulnerability of the latter.

In two ways, a backdrop based on historical values can sometimes be unobtrusively combined with the modern expression of these themes. The underlying balance of the traditional garden format has a familiarity to the eye of most

beholders that suggests its own timelessness. With such a perception, the landscape can have sympathy and respect for the ornament that attempts to transcend the time-scale in search of underlying truths. The second way is exemplified in those landscapes where the organic bones are in overt subservience to the focal point, anticipating and encouraging the bold statement. They contrive a harmony, without bias, between a strong subject and its surroundings; and whatever the tensions between the philosophical implications of the subject and the spirit of its surroundings, a unity and clarity of composition can be achieved. The ornament itself may beg questions of taste, but the combination is often able to avoid restless contradictions of style.

To reconcile contrasting historical truths with modern circumstances is a challenge widely experienced by today's garden owner. This would be less of a hurdle if private commissions were more commonplace. A perceived shortage of time, money, available expertise and artistry has made it unfashionable. At the moment, it is especially unfortunate that the private commission as an option does not warrant greater consideration and more enthusiastic exploration. The present huge demand for garden ornaments has lead to a noticeable renaissance of artists and craftsmen. Everything from ancient to modern, and from reproduction and 'in the style of' to fresh originality is on offer. Craftsmen would not be flourishing as they are if their services were geared and priced exclusively for the élite. The market has grown in leaps and bounds, reflecting needs and creating opportunities of supply at all levels.

Owners will not always commission a designer. But only by doing so will they avoid those compromises that off-the-peg purchases inevitably entail, and achieve the expression of both their own personality and that of the site.

This remains an age, essentially, where the whole is often the accumulation of disparate elements. The chances of an imbalance of composition are undoubted. However, there is also an increasing wealth of contemporary craftsmen, and an impressive range of available ornamentation that is both versatile and, to an extent, highly mobile. The modern garden, furthermore, often allows an ornament's immediate surroundings to be manipulated for its benefit. Thus there are ample opportunities for initiative and inventiveness in meeting the challenges.

Establishing roles

The visual strength of ornaments in the landscape must not be underestimated. By their nature, they can press a definition and focus on to a garden, transforming the scenery and disguising the unsightly.

The eye-catching qualities of the garden ornament are due only in part to the ornament itself. Whether as an attraction or a distraction, its prominence is greatly increased by the fact that it is an inorganic adornment to a largely organic environment. A certain potency, even excitement, is derived from the juxtaposition. The ornament projects a strength beyond its own inherent proportions. The reverse is equally true. A single plant in a plantless environment will assume an importance out of proportion to its size – for instance, a tree as the focus of a city courtyard or a strategic flower-arrangement or potted plant inside a house.

The ornament embodies a solid permanence in a setting where everything else, from the grass to the sky, is in a constant state of change, much of it uncontrollable and some of it unpredictable. A garden can take on very different moods, not only in the long term with the passing of the seasons and the passage of the years, but daily and momentarily with vagaries of weather. Man can help or hinder parts of the process and hope to gain a degree of control; but in the end he has to submit to Nature's authority.

Ornaments symbolically defy the forces to which their surroundings are subject. Hurricanes, drought, hard winters and disease can sweep through a landscape, but ornaments reward their owners with an immunity to such rigours, their visual presence constant and reliable. They imply immortality in a mortal world. Much, however, will depend on the choice of material, its durability and suitability to a given climate, and its upkeep. These responsibilities rest with garden owners, and the extent to which Nature has an impact on the destinies of ornaments is governed by the owner's care.

A statue or sculpture is also in a sense a personal statement; it is entirely and irrefutably man's creation. Every curve and detail is deliberate, its style and presentation a reflection of human intent. The garden ornament is inevitably a declaration by the owner, possibly of philosophy or more simply of taste.

In today's garden space is too precious to waste. It is important clearly to establish the purposes of each ornament. Random and hotchpotch siting, without due regard for such matters, can produce a superficially pleasing picture but can easily result in a meaningless jumble.

The main focus

The first decision in any garden is to select the focal point, whether of a single scene, a whole garden or a more extensive view. The eye of the beholder should be naturally drawn across the intervening ground towards the focus, and there it should feel justified in coming to rest. The successful focal point should give the complete picture an easy and convincing context, with proportion, definition and a certain finality. It need not necessarily be anything purely aesthetic; an attractive garden seat or pretty summerhouse, with their eye-catching qualities and clear embodiment of both rest and finality, will do perfectly well.

Traditionally, such logical conclusions are reinforced by symmetry and/or a perceived natural order; the ornamental focus may stand at the end of an axis, or centrally in some rounded or square area, or be placed carefully in tune with the pattern of a flowing landscape. It reflects, incorporates and finally appears to control and assume responsibility for the underlying balance.

Many modern gardens have symmetrical confines that are either immediately visible or clearly implied. If the focal point is to bring a convincing logic and harmony, its position should reflect and complete the proportions of the scene. Where, for instance, a garden runs away from a house, unavoidably in the shape of a rectangle, a suitable ornament placed centrally at the far end will appear to justify and conclude both the intervening ground and the configuration of the garden's

It is not enough simply to provide a large and striking ornament towards the end of a vista if it does not satisfactorily conclude that vista. At High Wardington, Oxfordshire, the eye may be confused, the urn attempting a main conclusion that is more convincingly found in the landscape beyond.

limits. If well chosen and well sited, the focal impact of the ornament can set the context to which other features seemingly subscribe; even obtrusive boundaries can be absorbed, serving rather than dominating.

As has been suggested, there should be a pleasing finality to a main focus that attracts and holds the viewer's attention. It is, therefore, important that such a point does not obviously break a line of sight at an intermediate stage. Stopping the eye without concluding the natural progression of the surroundings can appear contrived and meaningless. The eye wants to go on and feels unfairly arrested.

This century has seen a greater willingness to place main ornamental focal points in ways at variance with traditional concepts. They may be asymmetrical, co-ordinating a sequence of open spaces and planting, or light and shade. They may go further, defying any hint of belonging to a natural progression of the setting, aiming to grab the eye and startle the senses. Instead of invoking feelings of harmonious integration through symmetry and order, ornaments are used to provoke and challenge. Emotional and visual familiarity can be shaken and stirred, formality mocked and orthodoxy reinterpreted.

Such challenges are legitimate where the perceived role of an ornament is the asking of questions, rather than the providing of answers. The garden owner may be searching for reaction, puzzlement and introspection instead of harmony, logic and conclusion. Boldness of thought, however, is more easily acquired than the instinct and skill needed for successful implementation. If the definition radiating from the focal point is at odds with the natural definition of the setting, the former must have sufficient strength and impact; its presence should either dominate, or be easily grasped within, the contrary ambience of the setting. Without such power and clarity the beholder is likely to dismiss the picture as meaningless. If the eye is not drawn and held, it fails as a focus.

Problems of scale

A second very important role performed by ornaments is that of supporting the main picture. They help in the presentation of a view, guiding the eye forwards with a harmony and proportion that is appropriate to the focus beyond. The line of sight may be flanked by a pair of statues; it may have to start across a terrace or travel through an archway, both of which can be embellished with finials and other details; there may even be a wrought-iron gate that falls across the eye's path, imprinting its pattern on the rest of the picture without actually blocking it.

The more such ornaments intrude on the natural momentum of a line of sight, the more they detract from its conclusion. Normally this is detrimental to the cohesion and balance of a scene. There are also circumstances, however, where intermediate distractions can be used to good effect.

Modern gardens highlight both the problems and the potential benefits of ornaments in this supportive role. Shortage of space encourages a density of input and detail, and the ground that comprises the main or only view may also have to accommodate a wide range of other aspirations and activities. Thus, across a line of sight, there might be pergolas and pools, compartments and divisions, steps and junctions with other paths, and areas for rest and recreation. All these must be allowed their own levels of elegance, albeit modest. The danger is that the combined effect of the supporting cast, or the undue prominence of one of its members, may detract from the total effect.

There are often difficulties, today, in choosing the correct scale and style of ornament as a suitable focal point for the proportions and character of a particular garden. If the choice is not totally successful, the focus itself becomes a potential source of visual imbalance. In this situation, distractions and episodes can be deliberately introduced on to the line of sight in order to alter the perception and impact of its conclusion.

Side-shows

The third purpose for which ornaments are regularly employed is the provision of side-shows away from the main picture. From the central vantage point, such secondary attractions ought, initially, to be barely discernible if not completely invisible. They are creating self-contained scenes in their own right and need to retain some independence to avoid confusion. To the beholder, hints of delights yet to come will tempt the eye to enquire further, and encourage the feet to follow. Moments of excitement and interest can be held back to refresh and reward the curious.

Ornaments used in this way are able to introduce variety without disorder or chaos. The predominant spirit of a central area can, in the wings, give way to contrasting moods such as tranquil seclusion, intimacy, mystery, humour or irreverence.

The concept of a garden as a series of comparatively independent scenes united around strong, simple axes has recently become an established tradition. In Britain, Hidcote and Sissinghurst illustrate the success with which disparate themes can be incorporated into a cohesive whole. They may be interconnected, but the impact of each is kept within its own bounds and the essential bones of the main design remain free of clutter and fuss.

Size is certainly not a prerequisite for such an approach. A long, thin urban garden of mean dimensions may seem to be stuck unavoidably with one perspective. The idea of secondary scenes could appear to be wishful thinking, the owner becoming resigned to a garden that can be comprehensively read in a single glance, without venturing outside the window. Such despair, however, is unnecessary. Trellis work can be used to create lateral recesses and compartments whose contents are hidden from the house; archways and pergolas can be introduced to reinforce these sections without breaking the main line of sight; initially invisible niches will exist on the blind sides of evergreens. Both into and on to all these, there is scope for ornaments and ornamentation to be running their own small side-shows. Even the inevitable terrace or hard area adjacent to a house will often have one wing, subsidiary to the rest of the picture, where an attractive bench can become the focus.

Incidental detail

Smaller ornaments are used as incidental details, brightening up a foreground or functioning discreetly in a background. They can be extremely trivial and indicative of an owner's whims; hence the popularity of animals, such as pigs, squirrels and hedgehogs, cast in stone. Gardens have generally become more intimate and personal than in the past, being viewed as outdoor living-rooms as much as design show-pieces. Curios that just happened to appeal, and mementoes reminiscent of distant times and places, are more easily accommodated in today's landscape.

As with miscellaneous collections of pots, urns and other containers, incidental ornaments may also be made to serve a purpose. Plants gush forth from every sort of receptacle, and many bear witness to the inventiveness and creativity of the modern garden owner. Seventeenth-century cisterns no longer collect and hold water but tumble with a profusion of seasonal colour; chimney-pots, hollow plinths and a host of diverse objects are similarly exploited for their alternative uses. Glazed oriental pots, such as the large Chinese egg-containers, have not only been employed for planting but also as pools for wall-mounted, spouting masks and fish.

Where the incidental becomes, perhaps unintentionally, a strong focus in its own right, projecting an impact or style at variance with the rest of the garden, it is miscast. Its site and role need reconsidering.

Objects of no particular interest in themselves can often enliven the garden scene, like this plain stone bowl at Sutton Place, Surrey, used to receive water from a mask in the wall.

Adorning the functional

It has become an increasing preoccupation of modern garden designers that functional items should also be given an ornamental role. Everyday requirements are, more and more, transformed into or disguised as picturesque elements. Even where they can initially be kept out of sight, they can rarely remain entirely out of mind. Whether they appear as regrettable intrusions, detracting from a happy scene, whether they blend harmlessly, or whether they actively contribute to the visual pleasures in their own right, will depend on how sensitively both they and their settings are handled.

The proximity and pressures of the outside world render the defensive and screening qualities of a garden's perimeter particularly important. Dangers from marauding animals and unruly vagabonds have been replaced by the threat to privacy. High barriers are an effective answer but they are unhappily suggestive of a prison yard. Fencing, trellis-work (with or without fencing), railings and other metalwork are acceptable alternatives. Either on their own or in conjunction with existing walls, they combine efficiency with a wide choice of possibilities. This choice should be adequate to ensure some sort of aesthetic harmony, be it simple or fanciful.

Gates, gateways, doorways and alleys similarly need not be intractable elements in the smaller landscape. They can be the excuse for all sorts of ornamentation and embellishment, including wrought iron and overhead structures in wood. Alleys, especially, and the awkward spaces created by house extensions, are too often seen as no-go areas for artistic endeavour. Many may be unsuitable for general planting but they need attention because they lie uncomfortably close to the house and its windows. Modest pergola effects, arches, wall-masks, statuary and pots might be ingredients of a possible face-lift. If such settings are reasonably separate from the main view, fresh moods can be struck.

Blank walls can be cheered up solely by adding trellis running flat against them. Trellis-work comes in different shapes, sizes and grades of mesh, some being more ornamental to the eye than others. Diamond mesh and smaller grades have, perhaps, a greater decorative impact where the surroundings are solidly dominated by the straight lines and right angles of buildings, walls, windows and drain-pipes. It is dangerous to generalize, however, as each situation and its owner will have their own requirements.

Bleak stretches of masonry can be given more than just the simple mesh pattern. Both the trellis and the wall can, in theory, be painted with any combination of colours. One of the elements may be white while the other can either remain natural or take on a tone to suit the need of the site — from the subdued to the cheerful . . . or outrageous. It might be appropriate to choose a scheme in harmony with the room from whose windows the finished result will be enjoyed. These awkward areas, tucked between buildings and perimeter walls, often feel more a part of the house than of the landscape, and in need of inspiration beyond the horticultural. Outdoor paints and stains have improved considerably, so maintenance is no longer such a regular chore.

Garden furniture and summer-houses are further practical features that demand thoughtful handling. Whether immediately visible or tucked away, they ought to comprise at least a hint of the picturesque. If they and their surroundings have no respect for each other a whole scene can be spoilt. To suffer a permanent visual imbalance for the sake of an occasional practical use seems wasteful. It should, anyway, always be possible to utilize them as moments of interest, their patterns and proportions often being suited to focal points, flanking features or

The garden gate beckons the visitor's steps to enter. At Great Dixter, Sussex, Edwin Lutyens designed a gate whose rustic character is a prelude to the informal path of randomly laid stones, its edges softened by flowers. Such an approach, while not suitable for an imposing classical monument, is ideal for the understated and intimate ornament.

subsidiary roles. Where their character lacks decoration or charm, the manipulation of the immediate planting may more than compensate. A later section is devoted to this tactic.

Sheds and garages are easy recipients of trellis-work, and car-ports can be successfully transformed with pergolas ranging from the rustic to the formal. All these can carry both embellishment and planting to engender the desired atmosphere.

Conventional swimming-pools are often difficult to integrate into a landscape. The stirring prospect of statuary emerging from the watery depths is precluded where pool-covers have to come on and off. Spouting figures can, however, discharge from a safe spot. Water, anyway, is an attractive prelude to the view of any ornament set beyond, and this, at least, gives clear aesthetic overtones to the purely practical.

Permanent barbecue sites and sandpits are greater tests of ingenuity. Their potential for ameliorating ornamental detail may seem slim, but where they occupy prominent ground it must be worth exploring. The simplest and smallest of adornments might swing their visual balance from the abrupt to the harmless or cheerful. The geometry of both features may be suited to modest, rounded finials; or their starkness might be disarmed with animals and other figures in stone or lead. Storks and cranes cast in lead are a delightful mixture of modesty and elegance.

Preludes

Understanding the nature and potential of the various roles available to ornaments within any landscape, is fundamental to a successful design. The pattern of these roles is essentially constant whatever the context. One might be looking at a broad sweeping view, or a roof garden; one might be establishing the garden's single and only ornament, or linking a series to compose one picture or a cohesive progression of pictures.

The first requirement, undoubtedly, is a co-ordination of scale. Given the visual strength of garden ornaments, scale has to be handled with care. It is one of the easiest aspects to misjudge or ignore, and is a common cause of disappointment. Today's garden-owner does sometimes commission an ornament of the perfect dimensions to fit a specific role in a specific setting; more likely, though, he or she browses through a selection of various shapes and sizes, and buys ornaments originally meant for quite different roles. Ideally one would like to remove half a dozen and see how they look in their intended setting. Their implications could be seen by the eye rather than guessed in the imagination, but this is not often practicable.

Price and immediate impulse very often dictate a choice. The ideally proportioned urn, for instance, may be unaffordable; or one may fall head over heels for something irresistible but not suitable for its destined position.

It is essential to keep a critical attitude. Is an ornament cast in the right role given its scale relative to the site? Could it give an improved performance in that role with a little manipulation? Sometimes one can adapt lines of sight and setting to bring a landscape into balance with an ornament. The first consideration, however, should be that the ornament match the landscape.

The under-scaled

The role of the focal point is to draw the eye over the intervening ground. Too modest a statue or too small an urn may be unequal to the task. One should first consider resiting it in a supportive or secondary role, and replacing it by an ornament exerting more impact.

If this is impractical or if, for sentimental reasons, the idea simply cannot be entertained, the weak character might benefit from a helping hand.

With a successful co-ordination of scale between water and ornament, even the most contrived pools can take on a natural charm: Hazelbury House, Berkshire.

Plinths, for example, can give prominence to the slight or low ornament, raising it, perhaps, from below waist height up to a level with the eye. They can be of the simplest construction, and remain either visible or invisible. Where the market does not offer a ready-made plinth of the right dimensions, they can be made fairly cheaply from bricks, stone slabs or concrete, the latter either in block form or poured. Pointing and/or rendering may be necessary, but a degree of crudity is excusable if evergreen shrubs and climbers are going to hide the plinth throughout the year. Ivy, especially, will romp happily over such structures, leaving the eye to be drawn to the focus above. In open situations, plinths of a more gradual appearance can be fashioned with earth which is then either planted or grassed.

Scale will invariably be a problem where the main focus is low to the ground, unless it has some other inherent power as compensation. Increasing the height is one solution as long as the prop does not prove a distraction. If it looks contrived, mask the contrivance. If the overall impact remains weak, reconsider a fresh site where the scale is more appropriate; if no other ornament for the main focus can be found, use something else, such as a garden seat, or something organic, such as a plant, shrub or tree.

Where the problem is marginal, and an ornament only just lacks sufficient presence, an interesting variation of the plinth concept is worth exploring. Rather than increasing height relative to surroundings, one can use a change of material, or pattern, to distinguish the specific patch of ground on which it rests from the general run of ground that it commands. The patch can be flush with the ground; it can be raised in the manner of a low, wide plinth; or even sunk — as long as it is oriented to the desired focal point, clearly directing its impact and avoiding confusion.

This technique has many applications. On a terrace, for instance, where there is a predominance of stone or pre-cast slabs, an ornament intending to give character and focus may seem smothered if it is in a visually similar material. A pattern, perhaps simply a square, of cobbles or brickwork, under and around that ornament, might restore the cutting-edge to its definition. With sensitive handling, many combinations are possible. Stone can be introduced into brickwork, and vice versa; granite setts can be used in stone work, and vice versa; cobbles can be introduced into all three, though the opposite does not always hold; and any of the above could be used to lend presence to an ornament in an area of grass or low planting. Pebbles and gravels, in contrasting tones and grades, are also potential ingredients.

Play of patterns focuses the eye and creates mood. The composition at Dumbarton Oaks, Washington (below), uses a variety of materials including cobbles and stone slabs. At Meadowbrook Farm, Pennsylvania (right), the effect is more relaxed. A circle of bricks creates a calm space, from which the eye is led back through the wrought iron gate flanked by animals to a vista of alternating light and shade. Opposite below: Hazelby House, Berkshire, and Barnsley House, Gloucestershire, where ornamental buildings are subtly placed in surrounding planting.

The heavy lines of large tubs can be masked with profuse planting. Thus exploited, the nondescript can produce the eyecatching (Ilmington Manor, Warwickshire). At Brook Cottage, Oxfordshire (right), a low square plinth adds prominence by separating the spectacle from the surrounding ground.

The versatility with which both these and other elements, such as grass, planting and water, can be combined allows a wide range of effects. Patterns designed to draw the eye on to the ornament can extend further into the setting. It must be stressed, however, that while reinforcing and sharpening the focus is appropriate in alleviating marginal weaknesses, they can make serious deficiencies of scale even more conspicuous.

Water is possibly the most successful medium in the garden for isolation and highlighting. When correctly proportioned, it can endow an ornament with presence way beyond its actual size. To deprive such characters of their watery surrounds in favour of grass, paving or whatever, would leave many of them looking woefully inadequate. The immense potential of water is often under-appreciated because it seems unobtrusive, but there is hardly anything that can set off a focal point so vividly. In this respect, many swimming-pools represent missed opportunities; they are ideal for statuary in the water where practical, otherwise for something eye-catching beyond, be it simply an attractive garden seat.

The difficulty with water, in terms of garden design, is establishing the correct proportions. Its scale should complement both the ornament and the setting, with all three in harmony and the whole picture relaxed. There is a tendency in the modern garden to allow the water to be overshadowed by one, if not both, of the other two. The visual effect is contrived and far from convincing. When successful, though, water can take on a deceptively natural air, even where it does not pretend to be anything but man-made.

The over-scaled

The opposite problem is ornamentation that feels over-scaled for its setting. Disarming grandeur, however, to achieve a delightful understatement is usually considerably easier than mobilizing and re-equipping the weak. If there is a moral to this, it is: err on the large side when choosing a focal point, even where affording the size involves a compromise on quality. The perfect scene is more readily grasped with a scale that is veering towards the excessive, than with something that is hopelessly small. Deficiencies of quality can be disguised or compensated more easily than deficiencies of size.

Many of the solutions for the over-scaled lie in the stage-management of the landscape, and its ability to soften and partially obscure lines with shadows and planting. For the moment, though, let us consider the changes that can be wrought without disturbing the natural setting.

The option of a fresh site more suited to the ornament's proportions should be considered, not that this is a likely solution where it is already prominently placed as a main focus, in the middle of the stage. If this fails in its theatrical effect, the only solution may be to recast the drama, creating a largely invisible side-show for the prima donna.

The over-scaled ornament can perhaps be made a receptacle or vehicle for planting, thus providing its own disguise and deception. Bullish urns and out-sized troughs can be laden with planting that expresses a restrained or gushing informality. Their large dimensions, in promising a good root-run, can be the means to their own obscurity. Excessive lines can be lost under trailing geraniums with *Helichrysum* and the small variegated trailing *Nepeta* thrown in for good measure. More permanent camouflage is offered by a wide range of plants, including the various ivies, periwinkles, and Lamiums, *Cerastium tomentosum, Aubretia, Lithospermum, Arabis, Rosa nozomi, Euonymous fortunei* and *Cotoneaster dammeri, Artemisia, Convolvulus cneorum, Cistus* and *Cytisus x kewensis*. There should be sufficient diversity to realize the intended effect within the prevailing horticultural conditions.

Climbing plants are important; they can trail down from ornaments that are natural containers, and can creep up those that are not. Again, there should be enough choice between the delicate and the rampant, the deciduous and the evergreen, the sun-loving and the shade-loving, and so on, to achieve an aesthetic balance for the ornament's proportions.

Trellis and structures

Climbers and ramblers are also the vital ingredient of trellis-work, arches, pergolas and arbours, and the obvious option for other structures such as summer-houses. Where such features are endowed with pleasing scale and style, the planting ought to remain respectful and complementary, and refrain from depriving them of their character altogether. If, however, their weight and shape is absurd, and their impact incongruous, the obscurity of a jungle can be beneficial. Disappointing dimensions will not be noticed if they carry ebullient passengers. The stronger species and varieties of roses, honeysuckles, clematis, vines and ivies might suit; and there are also jasmines, actinidias, wisterias and the climbing hydrangea.

In urban and close-set suburban gardens, all these structural features are likely to need at least a degree of cover. Trellis-work, for instance, is at its most vital as a front line protection of privacy and seclusion, its climbers adding to the cover it provides. More important, though, is the aesthetic appeal of contrived and solid garden constructions, with their uprights and cross-pieces, in a landscape already dominated by other, larger structures. In these circumstances, the garden structure must, whatever its embellishments, be placed firmly into the context of the garden. The harmony and contrast derived from the planting it supports should ensure a structure's contributing to the ambience of a garden and prevent any unintended echo or prelude to the rigid lines embodied in buildings beyond.

Wood *is the most adaptable of all materials in the garden. Left: a modern version of a Jacobean gazebo at Old Westbury Gardens, Long Island. Above: Tyninghame, East Lothian. Here the wood is less obtrusive, a mere frame for the roses running rampant round the arbour in which the statue nestles. Below: a beautifully proportioned bridge at Pusey House, Oxfordshire.*

The formal, clear-cut lines of steps at Meadowbank Farm, Pennsylvania, are softened by the ivy trained across the risers, making the staircase part of the natural as much as the man-made environment.

Steps and water

Two other ornamental features can carry their own planting and so alter the perception of uncomfortable or excessive scale.

Steps and half-landings can have their proportions softened with comparative ease. Pots and assorted containers, overflowing with plants, might mask the wings; from cracks and joints can issue polite, little creeping characters, or more vigorous sprawlers; climbers, with nothing to encourage them vertically, can tumble downwards; ivy can be trained along the risers; and, if feasible, grass treads can be introduced. The impact of strength and shape can be much reduced even if some of their lines remain evident. Steps that were once broad, heavy and depressing appear more inviting to the eye with a leaner, narrower and less severe definition.

Pools and stretches of water offer the same option. If their dimensions are pleasing there is no harm in allowing the surface and outline to keep a sharp, unbroken clarity. But water that is too small either for its setting or for certain ornaments leaves little room for manoeuvre. The short answer is to enlarge it, but if that is impossible, one can look for a smaller ornament that still suits the setting; or try to relandscape to give the pool a more intimate context without spoiling a larger scene. If the scale is too large or too prominent, planting can be introduced to good effect. Water lilies can bring character and contrast to the surface, and irises can both flourish along the edge, interrupting its line, and jostle around any ornaments. A number of attractive water plants may be used, but where they tend to be invasive, they have to be severely controlled; otherwise the water may completely disappear from view.

Three more instances of sensitive planting softening the line of architectural features. Above left: the sides of a low flight of stairs at Dumbarton Oaks, Washington. Above right: plants around the edge of a pool, almost concealing it, in another Washington garden. Left: Pepsico, New York; here the influence is Japanese, contriving a strong contrast between the rectilinear pool and bridge and the sprawling shapes of the lilies.

179

Ornament creates mood. The great 'Gothick' trellises at Abbot's Ripton Hall, Cambridgeshire (below), stand free of planting, blatantly dominating the whole scene. At Sutton Place, Surrey (right), on the other hand, much simpler trellis shapes, covered in creepers, evoke a sense of mystery. Opposite below: an intriguing pergola more successful than the seats beneath it; and Kingsmead, Gloucestershire, the simplest form of pergola – a few poles and chicken wire – but effective in creating contrasting shade along the line of sight.

Techniques of enhancement

Ornaments and ornamentation, as we have seen, sometimes play a purely subsidiary role to the main focus. In most circumstances, they are simply delights to be enjoyed along the way, without providing the momentum and the destination. It is important that these intermediate adornments and details neither confuse nor totally stop the eye.

The middle ground of a line of sight is not always, however, as simple as it seems. It may have to be used in a variety of ways, practical and recreational; it may fall across areas of a garden that have contrasting moods and dimensions; or it might be designed to improve the perception of the less-than-perfect end-piece. There are two common practices that have implications of scale and which deserve consideration because of their potentials and dangers. One is the treatment of junctions. The other is the manipulation of the eye in its passage down the vista.

Where a main line of sight is crossed by a second axis or path, the junction, being strategic, begs some sort of definition. It is tempting to place a single solid ornament at the central point of the crossroads, but this needs great care. It may boast a profile in a number of directions, but it also affects the perspective of the principal view, and perhaps others as well. Such intrusions on to the middle ground of a line of sight need to be deliberately thought through.

Both the crossroads and the central spot of a longer perspective embody forward-moving visual momentum. Neither can claim to be a natural conclusion. This suggests two valid options for a centrepiece ornament. It must either be scaled down to respect the underlying momentum, allowing the eye to glide on to the destination beyond; or it must be scaled up to become a convincing visual destination in itself, the eye happy to come to rest without agitating at being deprived of a further focus. In this instance, the ornament and the foreground alone constitute a view and its satisfactory conclusion. The presence and focus of the ornament must be stronger than any onward progress apparent in the landscape beyond.

What has to be avoided at all costs is the view-blocker, the ornament that obstructs the eye's natural momentum without justification. It spoils the balance, harmony and flow of an end-piece, neither supporting nor supplanting, but just getting in the way. As an obstacle en route to the obvious, it is visually irritating.

Where a junction or mid-point requires elegance and interest, but not at the cost of visual momentum, there are still plenty of possibilities for ornamentation and decorative detail. Statuary and urns can flank; structures such as pergolas, arches and open-sided arbours can frame; and across the centre of the view or views,

At Old Westbury, New York, the main focus is the Baroque gateway at the end; but in between, the eye is intrigued and delayed first by the flight of steps and then by an openwork iron gate. The gardens were laid out in 1906 by George Crawley.

Even a swimming pool can be integrated into the sequence of incidents along a vista. Here, at Meadowbank Farm, Pennsylvania, we look first past a circular pond with a fountain, then through a gap marked by urns on pedestals to a bright blue swimming pool and finally to a rather stark modern pavilion.

the eye can glide over water and other changes in pattern and substance. Much the most subtle in their subservience to the longer perspective are water and structures that frame. They introduce their own distinctive character, with contrasts of shape and style, light and shade, reflection and texture.

The second practice so closely linked to the question of scale is the provision of ornamentation that can similarly mould and flavour the middle-ground, without any threat to the focus beyond. Circumstances may prevail where the momentum of a line of sight needs to be tempered, the middle-ground slowing the eye and implying greater distance. The configuration of intermediate ornaments can be used to alter the perception of a focus, their scale and prominence crucial in definition but safe in contribution.

Flights of steps present an obvious means of governing the speed with which a view unfolds. As has been mentioned, they can vary in the way they are perceived; some ascend effortlessly, others are heavy, horizontal and solid. Water, both in surface and outline, also offers a choice, the eye either gliding easily over a smooth expanse, or pausing to take in a wealth of detail. Whatever their nature, though, the very existence of steps or water on a sight-line suggests distance. The focus becomes a little more detached from the foreground, and the eye's movement will slow as it is given more to absorb.

183

Contemporary images respond to the same landscaping devices, though the opportunity
has been seized more readily in America and Scandinavia than in Britain, France or Italy,
still in thrall to tradition. Above: Max Ernst's highly personal fountain at Amboise, on
the Loire, is an exception. Below: Faringdon House, a fanciful display rooted in Victorian
taste. Right: the superbly co-ordinated garden at Pepsico, New York; sculpture, trees,
plants and water lead to a higher vista where spray is caught in the sun.

184

Pergolas and open-sided arbours go further. They not only imply distance and detachment, but they reinforce them with a contrast of light and shade, and enable the conclusion to be displayed within the frame of their own shape. Thus, even where the scale of a focal point is inadequate in a more general context, it may be saved by the proportions of the structure through which it is viewed.

Also offering a predetermined frame, but introducing a more dramatic sense of detachment, are walls and hedges that fall across the middle-ground. Windows, moon-gates, arches and gateways concentrate the focus to the exclusion of all else. Where an open-patterned gate is used as a prelude, imprinting its motif on the view of everything that lies beyond, visual progress is tempered most of all. The end of the vista is perceived only in the context of the gate, but, as with all open patterns, the perception of the gate will itself be within the context of the back-drop. If either threatens to be too complicated, the other must compensate with undemanding simplicity.

Such intermediate ornamentation suggests a detachment between the main focus behind and the ground nearer to the viewer. When the focus is suffering an imbalance or deficiency of scale, the strength and consequence of intermediate characters can ease the immediacy of its responsibilities to, and impact on, the foreground.

Painswick Rococo Garden: an openwork wooden gate serves to mark a boundary but not to hide the view on the other side; the gate becomes part of its setting, its mundane function masked within an attractive guise.

Barriers that fall across a view, but allow a glimpse of delights beyond, can both provoke curiosity and enhance impact. The scale and setting of a focus can be defined or sharpened, improving its perception.

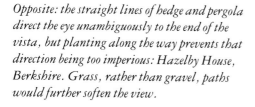

Opposite: the straight lines of hedge and pergola direct the eye unambiguously to the end of the vista, but planting along the way prevents that direction being too imperious: Hazelby House, Berkshire. Grass, rather than gravel, paths would further soften the view.

Water, *skilfully used, can give scale and even grandeur to features that would otherwise be insignificant. The small sculpture at Sutton Park, Yorkshire (opposite above), because it is set in the middle of a pool, makes an effect out of proportion to its size. Opposite below: intimate figures in intimate surroundings. At Reynolda House, N. Carolina, the combination of blues imparts a poetic ambience. At Saling Hall, Essex, the small figure is almost overwhelmed by jungle planting. Dumbarton Oaks, Washington (above), uses the device of narrowing the line of sight to create surprise. Water and urn are seen only when the visitor is almost upon them.*

189

Character and style

How we evaluate an ornamental feature will depend on the job we want it to do. The emphasis is not on its specific qualities as an *objet d'art*, but on its contribution to the scenery. At the same time ornaments often have a strong character of their own, and project that character on to their surroundings — sympathetic or argumentative, provocative or soothing.

Most garden owners want to imbue their ornaments with a sense of belonging or purpose, whatever the style. This, in turn, should lead to a clarity of both composition and impact. Such considerations can, however, be highly subjective, the assessment controversial, depending on the eye of the beholder. Every historical period seems to be available in today's wide range of ornament, garden design and backdrop. The backdrop may be beyond our powers to change, but whether or not it should dictate the nature of the garden design and ornament is a matter of dispute. It can be treated with respect or defiance. Certainly the extent to which classical design and statuary are employed in settings that are inescapably contemporary suggests that many garden-owners set, as it were, a false horizon at close proximity, and ignore the real one beyond.

The propensity for such defiance is more marked in some countries than others. Michael Lancaster, in an article lamenting the level of nostalgia in current English garden design, remarks:

'There is a suspicion of strong architectural form, equated with the new, the modern, which has permeated our society at least since the beginning of the 19th century (and many feel it to be justified in view of the recent failures of contemporary architecture). The British, it has been said, do not like things to look as if they have been designed, preferring them to look as if they have always been there; like the Aga cooker, old houses and mature leafy gardens.'

The physical landscape that surrounds the garden in modern Britain is often less significant than the emotional landscape that surrounds its owner. The latter is firmly rooted in a cultural heritage that survives in spite of change.

France, Italy and, to an extent, Germany have a similarly resilient tradition. Contemporary trends are less likely to diminish the private garden-owner's faith in ornaments whose subject matter and character are reminiscent of centuries past. The traditional and the familiar have a self-assured elegance and symmetry that communicates apparently timeless pleasure, and the fact that a setting is modern does not necessarily mean that it should contain modern sculpture. People feel uncertain about modernity; they do not understand it; often, paradoxically, they find it irrelevant to their own lives. The art form that reflects a contemporary context is not always the one that fits best into the emotional context.

Modern schools of thought, however, show a variety of response. Neo-classicists retain their essential loyalty but they combine it with new techniques and the expression of new moods to produce a distinct evolution from traditional classicism, reflecting the essence without being bound by the detail. Artists such as George Carter, Raf Fulcher and Elizabeth Tate have reinterpreted the classical, permeating it with a character and immediacy that is undeniably contemporary.

Others feel that any such loyalty to bygone concepts, however open to revision, is irrelevant. In today's context, classical elegance is viewed as a meaningless anachronism; not evolution, but a fresh approach is sought. Sylvia Crowe remarks that 'today the sculptor reflects the modern groping for the underlying unity of the world'. The breadth of concept and abstractions of form may well suggest this; but there is also a clarity of response in contemporary garden artform, both from the neo-classicists, and from artists working in more modern styles. These include Henry Moore, Eduardo Paolozzi, Barbara Hepworth, Jacob Epstein, Ben Nicholson, Max Ernst, Claes Oldenburg, George Segal, Larry Morris, Gerald Ogilvie Laing, Bruno Romeda, Simon Verity, William Pye, Gerda Rubinstein and Jack Lennor Larsen. Even deep-seated traditional prejudice can be disarmed.

Pepsico, New York, is notable for its bold use of modern sculpture (see overleaf). This group is by David Wynne.

Where contemporary sculpture does exert its magnetism over the beholder, the response is possibly deeper than the simpler pleasures provoked by unchanging classicism. The allegorical and philosophical content of the latter, while historically significant, is today less likely to stir profound emotion. As an art form in the modern garden, it asks little more than visual appreciation, and such undemanding charms will inevitably appeal to a wide audience.

Contemporary sculpture makes greater demands on the mind, but, in return, offers greater rewards. It may embody a spirit that is hard to define and yet difficult to resist. Semi-conscious emotions can be stimulated, deep-seated uncertainties revealed, and fundamental beliefs highlighted. The living artist has the opportunity to explore contemporary thought-processes, and communicate their insights.

Communication, however, imposes obligations on both sides. Where a statement is not immediately intelligible, the artist must accept and lead the receptive faculties of the viewer. If he or she remains baffled, the ornament has failed to transmit its meaning and has become simply a shape, to be enjoyed (or not) on visual grounds alone. Stark and abstract symbolism, if regarded by the beholder as nothing but decoration, can sometimes seem an uneasy ingredient in the lush, organic ambience of a garden. Yves Abrioux, who has strong feelings on the lack of sensitivity displayed by contemporary garden sculpture in France, identifies an 'arid modernism' that fails to take into account the 'rich texture of the setting'. Contemporary sculptures can, potentially, find a place in almost any garden, but where it fails to communicate its character and the meaning of its style, 'arid' is exactly the word for the bleak abstraction it conveys.

In some countries, notably the USA and Sweden, enthusiasm for concepts of garden ornament that diverge dramatically from the traditional has widened the popular perception of contemporary style and imagery. The wider sympathies and stronger demands that this has inspired, have created a healthy relationship between garden-owner and artist/sculptor. Ideas and their expression can be worked out mutually, leading to a flow of private commissions that is producing works to appeal specifically to the character of *this* client, *this* landscape and *this* moment in time. There is less tolerance for compositions that struggle to express themselves in irreconcilable historical conventions and greater confidence in a wholly modern vocabulary.

The ghostly presences that people modern gardens can be as varied and evocative as any in the past. The lady holding a basket of flowers at Barnsley House, Gloucestershire (above), is by Simon Verity. Opposite above: a modern totem, suggesting a carved stone in the Mayan jungle, in J.L. Carr's garden at Kettering, Northamptonshire; and an American Indian, perhaps the modern equivalent of Pan, at Brandywine, Delaware. Right: Claes Oldenburg's giant trowel and George Segal's spectral men and women on a bench at Pepsico, New York. Far right: abstract but scarcely less personalized figures by Larry Morris at Mr and Mrs Lapadula's garden, Washington.

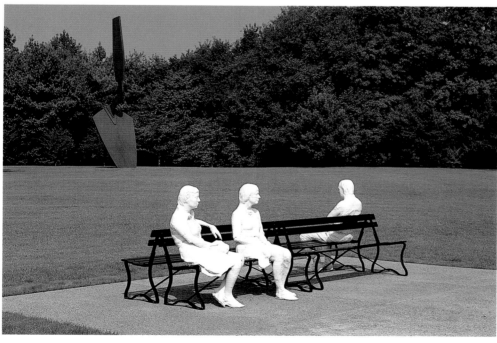

British gardens that have been transformed recently through private commissions for ornaments – Sutton Place in Surrey, designed by Sir Geoffrey Jellicoe and Sir Frederick Gibberd's garden in Essex, for instance – are still very much the exception. Many modern British sculptors are better known in the gardens of the eastern seaboard of the USA than in England. Britain, France and Italy, however, have to contend with the strength of ingrained historical tradition. It is right that superlative heights of garden artistry, inspired by the natural landscape, architecture and social fabric of previous eras, should be carefully preserved so that it can continue to be widely admired. Such outstanding moments become embedded in a national consciousness and militate against radical alternatives.

The advance of technology has been responsible for some novelties of expression, character and style. Its contribution is evident where light and water are harnessed to visual drama. The laws of nature can be supplemented or even spectacularly defied. Only rarely are they as subtly integrated as Toyo Ito's 'Tower of the Winds' in the Japanese city of Yokohama. This huge, perforated aluminium cylinder incorporates internal lighting effects that respond to changes in the direction and speed of the wind, the level of noise and the time of day.

Shape and detail

Within certain obvious limits, the shape and detail of garden ornaments have always encompassed a wide variety, and this variety has been increased by modern innovations. An ornament can be used to contrast with or to echo a rhythm inherent in the setting, its inorganic presence lending prominence and focus to a theme.

Vertical lines and profusion of detail suggest drama, movement and excitement. Horizontal lines and simpler detail incline to steadier feelings of repose and finality. Thus, where a view is naturally dominated by gentle, rounded shapes, from the foreground planting to tree canopies and a flat or rolling horizon, there may be an urge to introduce an ornament that offsets the tranquility. A vertically proportioned focal point, as long as it does not appear out of place, might invigorate the muted harmonies. Or an attractively embellished ornament might cheer up a bland and lifeless scene.

Contrasts must offset rather than upset. An infusion of ornate drama into quieter surroundings can in excess look pretentious, fussy or just plain ridiculous. Landscapes that carry their own balance of natural proportion and animation are more straightforward in their demands; statuary in such surroundings does not need to be exaggerated; they can also anticipate and accommodate a wide range of ornament, whatever their shape and detail. A deservedly popular sight is the iron seat that girdles a tree trunk. The strong vertical line of the trunk is balanced by the calm horizontal lines of the seat; the simplicity of the former should also offset the detail and pattern of the latter; both, hopefully are set under a rounded canopy of foliage, the natural proportions inherent in each producing a delightful mixture of contrast and complement. Creating interest for a setting, but also endeavouring to make that interest look completely natural, is a balance that is not easily struck.

Some surroundings – endowed, perhaps, with sharp silhouettes, intricate detail and firm vertical lines – are in themselves exciting. They may need, in fact, to be held in check by an ornament that exudes a powerful but disarming simplicity. Rather than seeking contrast, though, such a setting might build towards an ornament that provides the final exuberant climax. A substance that has the ability to induce either calm reflection or breath-taking excitement is water. Its shape and detail can be moulded to achieve the desired effect. It can soar proudly or burst forth in every direction; it can flow and fall gently along its course, amusing the ear as well as the eye; or it can be quiet and unruffled.

The impact of shape, detail and colour, and their projection towards the beholder, can be influenced to a surprising extent by the climate and geography of the setting.

Water, sculpture and clipped hedges are used to introduce severe drama into the natural landscape at Faringdon Park, Oxfordshire.

Higher latitudes, and regions regularly subject to cool temperate weather conditions tend to have a reasonably soft and grey light. Lower latitudes and hotter climates are the opposite, enjoying much sharper, clearer light. Comparatively short distances can separate areas that have significantly different strengths of light; the centre of France, for instance, is markedly clearer than Britain, and similarly Southern California as compared with the Northern Californian coast.

Where the light is softer, so, generally, is the perception. There is considerably more sympathy for ornaments with a gentle simplicity of line and detail. Modest and understated qualities, including colour, are presented more kindly and can even be flattered with a hint of restrained mystery. Their impact is enhanced, while intricate detail can become blurred and the extravagant lifeless. Strong colours, also, lose their vibrancy in softer light; they can look out of place where sunless days and misty conditions clothe the landscape with rich but endless variations of subdued tones. In a world where there is a complete spectrum of softly contrasting hues, and shadows of minutely differing depths, the quiet-spoken character shows at its best.

Sharper, harder light, as in the Mediterranean for instance, throws much sharper contrasts and gives much greater clarity to detail. Simple lines may look distinctly ordinary as they glare back at the viewer, but ornaments that carry elaborate detail will shine forth with high definition. The gloriously embellished splendour of many Italin statues is at its best where bright light and sharp shadows bring out every facet with maximum relief. The scenery can sparkle with a multiplicity of ornamentation and adornment without subsiding into a confused jumble. In softer light, their weaker projection sometimes has the air of faded grandeur.

Exactly the same principles apply to the artificial lighting of ornaments. Electricity offers comparatively inexpensive opportunities that can be exploited to the full in modern gardens. Prominent features are often within view of the house, and imaginatively illuminated they can still be enjoyed long after dark. Increasingly varied effects, furthermore, are offered by advances in lighting technology, from pencil-beam spotlights and low wattage systems to sparkler lights and fibre optics.

Sculpted animals have always been popular, sometimes as highlights in a layout and sometimes as incidental details merely reflecting the owner's whim. On the page opposite the two farther pictures are Meadowbank Farm, Pennsylvania, and Jenkyn Place, Hampshire; the three smaller ones Ince Castle, Cornwall; Kingsmead, Gloucestershire; and Marsh Lane, Harlow, Essex. Above: another part of Meadowbrook Farm.

Electric light offers new opportunities for displaying sculpture, but needs careful discrimination. Here Lord Leighton's 'Athlete Struggling With A Python' is lit in contrasting ways, producing very different effects.

Where the lighting is frontal it ought to be reasonably gentle for ornaments with modest lines and soft features. Stronger spotlights can leave restrained elegance horribly exposed, but they will thrill the more flamboyant type of ornament, which can appear pallid unless mood and detail are given sharp definition.

There are two alternatives to front lighting. The first, broken lighting, is almost always appropriate. Light may spill out from an adjacent uplit shrub, catching just part of an ornament. Some of its features will be visible, while others fade into semi or complete darkness, perhaps reappearing as a shadowy outline where light has spilt behind. The touch of reality combines, in the darkness, with a dramatic hint of mystery. It is quite possible for an ornament to look more impressive by night than by day.

The second technique concentrates entirely on proportion and outline. Instead of being spotlit from the front against a dark backdrop, the ornament itself is kept in complete darkness, its outline becoming a black silhouette, the lighting being used on the backdrop. If the backdrop is bland in texture, and the lighting restricted to a gentle wash across its front, the silhouette will take on a sharp, frozen definition. On the other hand, if the backcloth is angular, and uplights are used to throw deep shafts of light through a dark tapestry of patterns, the silhouette will be offset with less clarity but more mystery. The simplest of proportions, such as those of columns, repays this general approach.

It is all too easy to become carried away with garden lighting, the end-result being shop-window-style illumination that leaves nothing to the imagination. Too little is infinitely better than too much; and, for depth and intrigue, uplighting should always be considered before uncompromising, full-frontal spotlighting.

Colour, texture and repair

Colour is another characteristic that responds to different intensities of natural light. Softer light enhances softer colours, from the stone, marble and concrete greys, the weathered, sandy and buff browns, the various shades of wood and their stains, especially after weathering, to the paler terracottas and all the pastels. The appeal of stone, in its more subdued tones, is especially remarkable in reduced light; the variation in texture and blend of neutral colours even makes it difficult for wet weather to depress its personality. But, being the master of understatement, it functions less subtly in very strong light, losing depth and taking on a more oppressed and lifeless feel.

Brighter colours increase in vibrancy as the light sharpens. Much more suited to lower latitudes are white marble, white and whitewashed stone and concrete, all shades of terracotta and any of the more startling glazes, some of them hailing from Spain, Portugal and the Orient.

A tribe of terracotta pots in contrasting hues, scattered round a terracotta-tiled terrace with a stark white house behind, begs a bright sun beating down from a clear sky. Despite the strength of both competing and sharply contrasting colours, it becomes a cheerful and relaxed scene. Translated into greyer light, zest and charm would dissipate, the colours inclining to argument both between themselves and with their surroundings. Thus, a punchy-orange terracotta pot against red brick can seem uncomfortable in some regions, but combine with surprising warmth and harmony in others. Similarly, brilliant white Italian marble can sometimes seem to be leaping out of settings where greyer light predominates, only settling down and looking at home when sufficiently weathered. At this stage, however, the owner starts considering cleaning and restoration for the sake of its health. A more versatile white is Portland stone, with its softer tone and texture.

Darker colours can also claim a universal application. Lead, for instance, exudes strength and lustre under a bright sky and retains subtlety and interest elsewhere, its character blending sympathetically with other subdued tones. Not always, though, is it allowed to remain leaden in colour. An 18th-century fashion, reproduced by some 20th-century restorers, suggested that lead statuary needed painting. Either they were coloured entirely white, the smooth, unblemished texture that resulted having the sharp prominence of white Carrara marble; or, cheerful lifelike colours were used, overlain with a hint of classical theatre, the flesh pale pink, the hair flaxen and the clothes depicted as spun gold. In most landscapes and climates, and alongside other materials such as weathered stone, neither version of the fashion has often achieved sufficient harmony with its surroundings. Lead has enjoyed a more permanent popularity through its own natural colour and texture.

Where softer light prevails, and more brilliant tones appear obtrusive, the impact of conspicuously new materials can be disconcerting to the eye. Fresh stone or brickwork can thrust themselves forwards; recently created colour and texture can be disproportionately strong and distract from other qualities. British and many North American climates favour weathered tones and tradition reveres them. Ornamentation that suggests either a shop-window sheen or the standardized perfection of a model straight off the production-line is felt to be slightly vulgar and embarrassing.

Most materials can have their ageing or weathering process accelerated, especially where they are reasonably porous. Some stone companies offer to 'distress' a product before it leaves the factory, or sell proprietary solutions designed to give the same effect. Milk and yoghurt can be used, the older the better. Cow dung has its followers as a weathering agent. Others swear by mixtures containing coffee, tea or tobacco, all of which have staining qualities. If, however, the object to be treated is terracotta or red brick, dung and any of these last three can leave an unsavoury brown hue. Dairy-based products are probably better in such instances.

Cleaning is usually reasonably straightforward. Stone, brick, terracotta and wood will all respond to fairly mild cleaning agents, either from the kitchen cupboard or from a garden centre. A more drastic face-lift might be achieved with one of the acids available from builders' merchants for cleaning mortar. Advice should definitely be sought if there are doubts, and it is always wise, whatever the method, to precede a blanket application with a trial over a small area. Some terracotta, for example, can lose its colouring where too strong an agent is used; glazes and oil sealants can also be eroded, increasing porosity and the likelihood of frost damage.

Structural disrepair, as long as it is static and safe, may simply involve cement-putty being applied to cracks and fractures, its final surface perhaps incorporating grit or dirt to mask its freshness. Where restoration proves impossible, one can often manipulate the setting to distract attention from the problem. There are plenty of instances of statuary continuing to play an important role even after losing an arm or a leg.

Weathering has much to do with a statue's suitability, especially in a garden with a northern climate. This classical maiden, made of composition stone, has acquired an attractive patination of moss and lichen. Artificial means are often used to weather new stone.

The versatile urn *can assume an amazing variety of shape, silhouette, profile and decoration. It can be a dark form against light, or a light form against dark. At Sutton Place, Surrey (above), urns make a stately procession in a setting of formal hedges. At Chidmere, West Sussex (opposite upper left), the flower-filled vase seems puny in its monumental setting. At Beauforest House, Oxfordshire (upper right), the sequence of lit and shaded sections of the same path gives atmosphere and poetry. Opposite below: Sutton Park, Yorkshire; and Marsh Lane, Harlow, Essex.*

'Stage-managing' the surroundings

'Stage-managing' the surroundings to suit the ornament is one of the most useful tactics available to the modern gardener. An ornament will not always be perfect; it may be badly proportioned, or weak, or have some specific feature that needs masking. 'Stage-management' in the garden cannot do everything but it can do a great deal to help. Some ornaments are appallingly chosen. But something that seemed at first only vaguely suitable may be transformed in its effect, snatching huge pleasure out of mediocrity.

The line of sight is one of the most important ingredients of an ornament's impact, whatever the size and context of the garden. Its shape, style and detail govern the path along which the eye is drawn, and it is seriously at fault if it fails to do justice to its culmination.

Broad sweeping views imply strength or grandeur. They provide a natural setting for imposing ornamentation.

Where the length and breadth of the visual sweep are sharply defined, the focus is concentrated and its impact heightened. Tightly clipped hedging, such as yew, propels the eye rigidly to the end of the scene, a conscious and weighty contrivance that serves the conclusion with single-minded purpose. Such stark and blatant stage-management must be carefully aimed. One must be careful to avoid anti-climax. But such treatment is perfectly suited to the ornament that has undeniable stature or presence but perhaps lacks the ability to project its qualities over the required distance. The eye will feel rewarded, the strict discipline being justified. If the natural impact of the focus is already immense, and capable of commanding the distance unaided, the contrived approach will certainly lend drama. Overdone, it may go too far — melodrama rather than drama. Hedging may be allowed to assume a more relaxed feel as an alternative prelude to grandeur. Ageing yew, for instance, cut to undulating contours rather than a straight line, will offset the exuberant with less artificiality.

Pleached allées of hornbeam or lime retain clarity but are less uncompromising and flat than the manicured hedge. Although still very much in control of the eye's course, it will appear more relaxed. The contrast of trunk and leaf introduces a greater depth of light and shade. In every case, however, the finale has to justify the prelude.

Avenues offer further possibilities of defined breadth and sweep without theatricality. Some, such as hollies, *Quercus ilex* and bays, can be clipped (perhaps as lollipops) to suit the dimensions of a focus; with natural proportions more in evidence, though, they will not compel the eye as overtly as the allée or hedge. Avenues constitute a frame for an ornament, the width across the avenue, both at trunk and at canopy levels, and the height between ground and canopy, setting the dimensions. The type of tree chosen will suggest a certain style, and the planting density will help to create a mood.

An ornament making a majestic statement is enhanced if the eye approaches it along a solid, rounded and weighty avenue of broadly spaced oaks or chestnuts. Where the focus required the solidity but none of the majesty, the width of the avenue could be reduced, as could the spacings along each line, so that all the canopies meet. The effect will be softer, more shady, and definitely less imposing. Limes, beeches and poplars can produce graceful and flowing atmosphere and, although they still anticipate a conclusion of some strength, it need not be heavy or grand. Any of these three can be close-planted to create a dark, intimate but powerful setting, suited to the ornament, perhaps, that is slight in dimension but considerable in presence.

The variations are as numerous as the permutations of tree type and spacing. Almost any scale of ornament can be shown off to its advantage, as long as it is not too close to the ground. Character is more important: it must balance the strength that an avenue gives to a line of sight.

Double borders, and the path they flank, can also be varied in configuration to suit an ornament beyond. The broader the path, and the more sharply defined, the

Nude figure in fibreglass by Gerda Rubinstein, in the garden of Marsh Lane, Harlow: a traditional use for sculpture yet unmistakably modern.

greater the expectation of a strong conclusion. Similarly, broad beds that are full of clear contrast and emphasis will tend to raise anticipations of a powerful culmination. If the borders are composed of soft, flowing detail, with rounded shapes both merging into each other and largely obscuring the path edges, the eye will be drawn gently and prettily to what one hopes will be an appropriate focus.

Where the character of the middle-ground is disproportionately strong a simple urn, with no pretension or punch, will fail to compete as a focal point. It will also be a disappointment where a broad, sharply defined path has rushed the eye forwards, whereas a better balance would have been achieved had it been drawn gently. A statue bursting with grandiose strength, on the other hand, will look top-heavy if the line of sight is full of delicate understatement.

The element of recreation is probably more prominent in the small modern garden made for daily use than in the stately landscapes of the past made for show. But that element should not be in conflict with the aesthetic. Above: an ingenious moveable seat at Felbrigg, Norfolk. Below: a spindly iron seat somewhat at odds with a Jacobean balustrade at Charlecote, Warwickshire. Right: a Victorian seat of almost exaggerated richness but showing to ideal advantage against the plain dark hedge of yew; Brook Cottage, Alkerton, Oxfordshire.

At Sutton Park, Yorkshire, urns are used picturesquely. Here an urn provides a gentle and pleasing focus. The sequence of trees and hedges, patches of light and darkness, lends variety and interest to the view, though it is undoubtedly completed by a cleverly sited ornament.

Squeezing the view of an ornament into tighter dimensions not only increases the drama and sharpens the focus, it also implies a degree of modesty, allowing a brief glimpse of an intimate and private scene. The effect is similar to the introduction of a pergola, suggesting that the ornament is somehow in a world removed from the beholder, but nonetheless able to project its personality from a distance by virtue of the smaller frame. The squeeze to the sight line might only involve one point of the intermediate ground, using hedging or evergreen shrubs strategically to flank a path and reduce the visibility of anything beyond. This approach lends high drama to the stronger ornament and is an excellent option where the same figure is viewed from a number of different angles. If, however, this becomes the one and only vision of the mighty, there is a danger of it resembling a caged tiger, dramatic but out of place.

Introducing phases and episodes at mid-points along a view has already had some consideration. The eye can be slowed and amused on its travels, passing under pergolas and arches, up and down steps, over water, through gates and between pairs of flanking figures. Planting can deliberately encroach, and the ground might comprise a sequence of gravel, paving, brickwork and grass.

One of the most fundamental and effective of episodes on a line of sight is the contrast of light and shade. Its manipulation can appear completely natural, and yet produce moments of magical artistry. Darkness implies depth, distance and the unknown, putting any ornament that lies beyond into a separate context. Thus the eye can be given considerable pleasure if, as it moves along a view, it is led from light through darkness and on towards a focus that falls in a second pool of light. The travelling should be as much fun as the arriving. The distance over which this can be achieved can be quite short; one could rely simply on an archway, a single tree or a pair of evergreens to throw the necessary shadows. Pergolas and arbours are more comprehensive, maintaining the contrast in all weathers; and avenues offer a wider range of alternating, and perhaps ever-changing, pattern.

Ornaments with simple and elegant proportions and charming outlines are ideal candidates to conclude such sequences of light and dark. They might even be sited short of the final area of light so that only a silhouette is shown. Intricate and elaborate detail may become blurred, their finer qualities diluted over the real, or implied, distance. If the intended focus has few attributes, it might be better established in shadows beyond, reaping the benefit of the sight line's character but coy about its own.

Good light and no distractions allow perfect vision, the impact of any ornament accurately reflecting its exact physical appearance and inviting scrutiny. Half light and shade, whether dappled or deep, prevent such clinical assessment. An ornament that is not completely or clearly seen commands more powers of suggestion. The eye will have an impression of what is there, the sight-line and setting will add their own implications, but the imagination will do the rest. The over-sized, the under-sized and the disappointing can be cloaked in modesty or mystery. Their presence can remain strong and they can continue to perform an allotted role, but the disclosure of all their details is avoided. With shadows, and a little shrewd contrivance, the ugly duckling might even be mistaken for a shy swan.

The backdrop

Much of this section has been devoted to the strategic potential of the ground that separates the ornament from its audience, but its most immediate, organic surroundings are also vitally important. Exploiting or creating shadows over a site is just the beginning. The texture, shape and character of its closest neighbours have a bearing on the way an ornament is perceived. This especially applies to planting that directly comprises the backdrop. Different plants or, occasionally, the same plant with different treatment, can change the mood and projection of a figure, sometimes marginally, sometimes dramatically. A degree of imbalance can certainly be redressed.

So before wider and longer views are torn apart in the search for the perfect effect, more parochial solutions ought to be evaluated – just as it would be foolish to redecorate a whole room for the sake of a picture when a change of frame would suffice.

Plants, like ornaments, have their own distinctive proportions and characteristics; it should be possible, within the horticultural limits, to choose those that best set off a particular ornament and define its intended role. One may want a quiet, respectful backdrop where the planting appears subservient and the emphasis remains on the centrepiece; or, there might be a call for a more deliberate interaction, the planting making a definable contribution to our view of the ornament. If

the latter is disappointingly short of personality and style, a setting that has both in abundance may compensate; it can overflow with shadowy elegance and movement, giving the picture as a whole a character that it would otherwise lack.

Where a garden ornament is rewarding in its own right, all that may be required of the surrounding planting is a texture to act as a fairly neutral backcloth. After water and grass, clipped yew has been deservedly popular in this role, setting off statuary in the same way as dark velvet shows off jewellery. Its quiet depth and solid shape are perfectly muted within bland detail and subdued formality. The matt canvas it can provide throws the entire focus on to the ornament, crystalizing its detail and highlighting its drama with sharp relief. The grand, the ornate and the stylish will enjoy such settings, while weaker and quieter characters might be overawed, receiving little sympathy.

Yew, in its obedience to clipping, can display a further dimension. If the flat canvas is too bleak and the mood too frozen, it can be 'sculpted' to provide niches and recesses. Ornaments can be mysteriously emerging from shadowy depths.

Other conifers offer a range of both similar and contrasting character, colour and texture. Few, however, submit to the same degree of control over the decades and centuries.

There are plenty of plants that promise an evenness of texture through shaping but whose character is less formal. *Lonicera nitida*, box, privet and holly can be ruthlessly controlled; compared with yew, though, they display greater detail and lustre in their leaf. This projects a noticeably busier personality on to the backdrop, making them less suited to an ornament displaying a busy intricacy of its own. Their texture remains essentially flattering but its pattern softens the relief afforded to the focal feature.

All the above are evergreen and have the advantage of remaining constant as the months roll by. Deciduous candidates which perform a similar role are beech and hornbeam, which retain their dead leaves through the winter until the next year's growth is ready to appear. Both can be clipped into shape, and both offer a texture that is considerably less muted than yew. Always a part of their picture, however, are the seasonal tints of foliage, from lime green in the spring to rusty brown in the winter. Their fullness of character and progression of mood look best as a backdrop when the focal feature strikes a strong contrast, providing a firm context. It does not need to be grand or breathtaking. Beech and hornbeam suggest a gentler subservience that accommodates elegance down to a fairly modest level. The detail of their foliage, though, must not distract from the detail of the ornament.

Some of the larger-leafed evergreens can be moulded to form solid texture rather than individual outline. The different laurels are all good examples. They take less kindly to shears, and require a patient pair of secateurs where torn or amputated foliage proves unsightly. They are, otherwise, full of presence, their larger leaf pattern and darker depths giving a relaxed and kindly mood to accompany a wide range of ornamentation, however detailed. Where ornaments are sited in full shade, those laurels that have a noticeable shine to their leaves will provide a more cheerful backdrop than yew.

Should any of these evergreens be allowed to assume a more natural shape, weight and solidity would be retained but their stiff detachment as a backdrop would be lost. Apart from yew, box, privet, holly, *Lonicera nitida* and the laurels, there are others, such as camellias, rhododendrons and choisyas, that have their own varied attractions as well as acting as a setting for ornament. Gone is the

---

The art of garden ornamentation is to draw the eye forward, to excite but also to conclude, to guide but also, where necessary, to amuse and delay. In this vista at Meadowbrook Farm, Pennsylvania, the sequence of grass, gravel, stone and planting, the hint of as yet unrevealed excitements running across the main axis, the contrast of light, shade and levels, and, most obviously, the wrought iron gate, all provide intermediate interest that slows the eye and implies distance. The view, however, is not itself endangered.

White sculpture against a dark hedge – the perfectly calculated backdrop to show the marble bust to best advantage: Madresfield Court, Worcestershire.

backdrop of bland and contrived obedience. Gone is the isolated and clinical definition that it afforded. The ornament increasingly feels reconciled with, and a part of, the landscape's own free spirit.

Where a statue, urn or piece of furniture has a visible imbalance of scale or weakness of character, its impact may need further softening. Many of the above plants, grown freely, offer ample opportunity for sleights of hand. Their shapes produce more broken and deeper shadows. If necessary, wands of foliage can prevent an ornament from being seen in its entirety. These settings have the ability to cast obscurity in the most plausible manner, replacing a hard focus with an emergent mystery that is more suggestive than clearly defined.

It is not always essential to provide mass or solidity. Some plants are eminently suitable as neighbours because their own patterns of line and foliage echo, contrast or complement the style of the ornament. A statue or urn, for instance, that is predominantly vertical in proportion, or anything raised on a plinth, may be pleasantly offset by planting conspicuous for its horizontal tiers of growth. The partnership can be more than a mere mutual complement. The calming qualities of flatter lines can help to stabilize and anchor the momentum of a vertical form into its setting. Some of the larger shrubs suitable in this way are *Viburnum plicatum*, *Cornus controversa*, *Cornus kousa* and some of the *Mahonia* species. Of these, only the last are evergreen. On a lower scale, and especially for smaller statuary, and many plinths, the choice includes *Cotoneaster horizontalis*, *Hostas*, Solomon's Seal and, in the evergreens, *Viburnum davidii* and *Ceanothus thyrsiflorus repens*. Many of the Junipers are tiered, and their range, at maturity, can satisfy widely varying height requirements.

To echo predominantly rounded or horizontal ornaments with plants of a similar configuration needs care. It may be necessary where the picture already has an abundance of strong vertical lines, perhaps from clearly defined tree trunks or other planting, or from an urban or coniferous background. In this case, a low urn, eager to impress with expansive and flatter lines, may need to be reinforced as a focal point if it is to hold the whole scene together. Repeating the proportions in the immediate planting could produce the vital element of breadth.

If, however, the perspective is predominantly flat and rolling, such repetition may be cumbersome. Here the horizontally proportioned ornament may benefit from more vertical neighbours, and the one that is vertically proportioned will come into its own. Should it not be sufficiently forceful, one can devise planting that either anticipates or echoes. The anticipation should be forwards of the immediate planting, on the sight line, where opportunities may exist for evergreens clipped as pyramids and other vertical shapes. Echoing the vertical, furthermore, does not suffer the curdling repercussions of repetitive horizontality. Upward lines are suggestive of movement, and in combination they can produce enclaves of lively drama. There are many such moments to be enjoyed in Italy where statuary and cypresses soar together. If this is overdone, though, a landscape can begin to feel frantic.

Plants offer a wide choice of vertical lines. Tree trunks have the clearest definition and can be used as long as their proportions at maturity are considered in the context of the ornament's scale. It may be appropriate to close-plant a number of small-growing trees, in the manner of a grove, and preferably all of one type to give simplicity to the backdrop. Some trees also offer the options of distinctively patterned barks and autumn colouring, as well as the mixture of dappled light and shade. The companionable qualities of trees are more diverse than is often realized. Their dimensions and proportions can fit a wide range of settings, and fastigiate growth, to further emphasise the line of their trunks, varies in height from the Italian cypress down to the small, slim junipers that look like punctuation marks.

A classical statue at Anglesey Abbey, Cambridgeshire, gives a vertical accent to surroundings that are predominantly rounded.

Tree trunks are the most emphatic of verticals, equally effective as a backdrop or, as here at Marsh Lane, Harlow, as a foreground, throwing into relief the sunlit lawn beyond.

Flanking an ornament with herbaceous planting can also provide excellent vertical emphasis. One of the best is the iris, which retains its sharp lines for as long as it is in leaf. *Sisyrinchium*, *Kniphofia*, *Crocosmia* and *Hemerocallis* can also display pleasing upward bursts of foliage. Hollyhocks, delphiniums, verbascums and lilies command striking outlines when about to flower and during flowering; their contribution may be of a shorter duration but it can be memorble, and they are valuable companions to ornaments of all shapes.

Mention must definitely be made of the bamboos and ornamental grasses. They include a wide range of height, girth and hue, but more important is their dense mass of soft, tapering lines. As backdrops to ornaments, they combine simplicity with both delicacy of texture and reassuring strength. Indeed, they often make such a satisfying picture in their own right, that they can be uneasy partners to a poorly shaped statue or sculpture; they may, so to say, mock the afflicted rather than provide comfort and support. Otherise, bamboos and grasses can accompany a comprehensive range of ornamental styles, from ancient to modern.

One must never forget that however clever an ornament's surrounds are in texture or shape, if their detail distracts they are probably doing a disservice.

There are plants though, whose distinctive contribution is largely in the detail and pattern of their leaf. Their best effect is probably in the creation of contrast. Repetition is useful when both elements are simple but dangerous where both are intricate. Those ornaments with lines that are devoid of fuss or clutter are often flattered by foliage with a strong pattern of its own. The palmate leaves of tree paeonies and fatsias, the linear geometry of *Euphorbia wulfenii* and a host of others can introduce a level of elegance and decoration to the back of a picture that may be missing from its centre. Where the ornamentation, including furniture, carries its own elaborate detail, background foliage either wants to blend into a texture or suggest simple solidity, as with the hydrangeas and many evergreens.

Pinnate leaves, with their herring-bone configuration, are especially attractive in conjunction with the more contrived lines of ornaments, and are rarely distracting. Ashes, robinias, gleditsias, aralias and wisterias can provide such surrounds. Softer still are the plants that can produce a wispy effect, such as willows seen at a distance. *Tamarix pentandra*, artemisias and many of the other silver-foliaged plants can create lightly floating settings, full of movement and shimmer. Very heavy ornaments may look clumsy and out of place against a feathery backdrop, but those that carry their own simple elegance should be perfectly suited.

The way in which this fairly ordinary sculpture of a child is surrounded by such a lavish display of flowers and foliage gives it both charm and presence.

Variegated foliage can be confusing as it creates a unity of effect that needs no addition. It has an inherent balance and contrast of detail with which to catch the eye and can easily compete for attention with an ornament that has been placed there to make its own contribution. The mottling can also mar the clarity of an ornament's outline. Statuary that can enjoy and benefit from such neighbours is that which has strength, simplicity and a paucity of detail.

Garden furniture deserves special mention in this context of 'stage-management'. It has its own patterns, character and complementary proportions. They may be simple, they may be graceful and delicate, or they may be more heavily ornate. Only the plainest and most solid structures look their best against backdrops that seethe with hectic activity. Too often, the lines and ambience of a garden seat are lost in a blurr of rambled plants, as if it were there more or less by chance.

The pinnate leaves of the wisteria and a diversity of foliage in a random collection of pots makes an attractively informal background for this bust at Saling Hall, Essex.

Two ways in which careful planting can enhance sculpture and furniture. In both cases, the contrast in texture and colour gives the objects a clarity that they would lack on their own. Below: Nymans, Sussex. Right: A provocative combination of urn and bench enjoy high definition at West Green Park, Hampshire.

The planting behind garden furniture need not be quite devoid of pattern or character, but it ought to be deliberately complementary. Seats, and the like, are unavoidably eye-catching, being conspicuous man-made elements inserted into a natural setting. Furniture that is relaxed and simple in line can be beautifully offset without difficulty amongst more intricate patterns of shape and leaf. Where the intricacy is in the furniture's own ornamentation, it is important that the backdrop has an element of weight and texture. The picture suffers as a whole if neither complements the other.

Colour, also, can be important. If the furniture is pale and white it gains its sharpest definition against darker green foliage. If already dark in tone, it can either be given a brighter background for impact, or deliberately allowed to become lost amongst plants of a matching hue.

Where furniture is really too large for the site, 'stage-management' can only come to its rescue if there is sufficient space for the appropriate planting. This can be a problem in the small garden. Heavily over-proportioned furniture can flood across a scene in such an obtrusive manner that to soften or lower its profile with plants becomes an impossible task. It permanently dominates, eclipsing the picturesque. Outdoor furniture, however, is now offered over such a wide and comprehensive range that comfort should be achievable without the complete abandonment of the garden's aesthetics. At best, its presence can be made pleasing; at worst, quietly inoffensive. There are few excuses for anything less.

The inadequate or misguided use of what I have called 'stage-management' can be recognized by two contrasting but equally regrettable symptoms. One is when the ornament is insufficiently masked, spoiling the scene by being too prominent. The other is when that which deserves to be seen and appreciated has become lost in the setting, failing to contribute as much as it might by not being prominent enough.

As I have tried to show, both are unnecessary. Today's landscape is too precious to waste, especially when one thinks of how much pleasure it can bring.

*The Rosary at Ashridge, from Humphry
Repton's 'Fragments on the Theory and
Practice of Landscape Gardening', 1816.*

A SURVEY OF AVAILABLE GARDEN ORNAMENT

James Rylands

One of a pair of Georgian stone baskets of flowers
99 cm. 39 in. high

These intricately carved pieces were popular in the 18th and 19th centuries and used on terraces and balustrading.

THE OBJECTS ILLUSTRATED in this survey of garden ornaments are a selection of the sort of items available at auctions of garden pieces or else through specialised garden dealers. Care has been taken not to concentrate only on very rare and magnificent pieces which grace famous gardens around the world, but instead to show more typical pieces which are accessible to the collector of average means.

Most of the pieces in this section are not photographed in a garden but in a fairly neutral setting, since our purpose here is to concentrate on the objects themselves rather than their placing. In conjunction with the other sections of the book, this should stimulate the imagination since the aesthetic merits of the piece can be enhanced or devalued by the way it is positioned; the same garden temple lying mossy, broken and neglected in a builder's yard, can take on a new lease of life when the columns, their charm even enhanced by the damage, are placed with calculated informality as a ruined temple in an Arcadian setting in a garden or park.

Condition is obviously very important in assessing a garden ornament which is more prone to weathering and eventual decay than an indoor piece. Personal taste plays a large part in determining whether the weathering and perhaps damage to the piece adds to or detracts from its beauty. Ornaments are made in a variety of materials, each of which has its own properties and each of which ages at a different rate and in a different way. Particular reference has been made to this in the text accompanying the photographs since in choosing pieces for the garden it is important to consider the material and the speed at which pieces weather in relation to the climate in which one lives. Cast iron, for instance, over the years tends to become brittle and easily broken, whereas wrought iron, although non-rigid and more flexible, tends to be of thinner construction and thus more liable to rust. Both are usually painted, sometimes with many layers accumulated over the years. This often obscures the finer detail of the casting but can provide a very desirable finish where earlier layers of paint of the creamy emulsion type, quite often in greens, blues and white, are showing through. Sand- or shot-blasting pieces brings back the finer detail but when finished in a modern paint often looks very new and can seem more like a reproduction than an original. Preference of paint finish should be dictated by the eventual location of the pieces in the garden.

Ornaments in cast, carved and composition stone attract lichens and moss more readily than a smooth material. Those carved in softer mediums, such as Italian limestone, although very quick in acquiring a desirable weathered patination, will also eventually crumble through rain and frost in a Northern European climate. Conversely a piece in Portland stone, much favoured in the 18th and 19th centuries, takes longer to weather but is a more durable material.

The last few years have seen a marked rise in interest concerning garden ornament. This has led to fairly indiscriminate buying, since there has not been enough precedent to help buyers to be discerning in their purchases. One of the aims of these pages, besides showing a typical cross-section of what is available, is to comment on the rarity and desirability of some objects as well as giving some idea of how they were made, remembering at the same time that a piece does not necessarily have to be of great age or rarity to have aesthetic appeal and merit.

Architectural features

Cast iron garden gate
122 cm. 48 in. high

A good quality cast iron garden gate, c. 1860, which, although incorporating a number of elements of design, successfully combines foliate motifs with architectural elements.

Pair of wrought iron gates
335 cm. 132 in. high

These are loosely based on an 18th-century style but were produced early in the 20th century and are of considerably better quality than the average.

One of a pair of massive 18th-century cast and wrought iron entrance gates
435 cm. 171 in. high

Although of fine quality and magnificent proportions, the sheer size of these gates makes them suitable for only the grandest of residences.

Painted wood side or dog gate
91 cm. 36 in. high

An extremely rare example of an 18th-century wooden gate. It is constructed in the style of Chinese Chippendale furniture, more often associated with treillage in the garden.

Pair of 18th-century wrought iron gates
207 cm. 81 in. high

The quality of workmanship and design sets these apart from most 19th-century imitations. In particular the binding collars and the splaying at the ends of the scrolls are very typical of 17th- and 18th-century wrought iron work.

Set of four Istrian stone columns
300 cm. 110 in. high

Of Venetian origin, these could be purchased individually or in sets either to incorporate into architectural schemes or to place free standing in the garden. Many others now to be seen in gardens, however, have been removed from demolished buildings, and used to great effect in a garden setting.

Sandstone and marble table
367 cm. 144 in. wide

A good example of how redundant architectural fittings can be adapted for garden use. The base is made up of two pilaster capitals originally rebated into the wall at the back of a portico which have now had a large slab of marble placed on them, making an outdoor table.

One of a pair of rusticated Portland stone gate piers
360 cm. 142 in. high

Produced c. 1740; sadly only one of the pair survives. Despite being unable to fulfill its original function, this would still make a magnificent vista piece surmounted by the mask-carved urn.

Pair of 19th-century sandstone griffins
135 cm. 53 in. high

These have almost certainly been removed from the parapet of a large Victorian Gothic building. They would now look equally at home either surmounting gate piers or else flanking steps in a garden.

Three sandstone gargoyles
110 cm. 43 in. high

Although medieval in style, these would have adorned the corners of a Victorian building. They still have the stone rebate by which they would have been set into the masonry. It is redundant architectural fittings such as these which present the greatest challenge to the imaginative garden planner; they could be very effectively incorporated into a garden wall, or even placed partially obscured in a border. Compared to many other more traditional forms of garden ornament, redundant architectural fittings are still very cheap and can provide the most fun in incorporating them into a garden scheme.

Portland stone Composite order capital
85 cm. 33½ in. wide

Removed from the top of a column adorning a building, such capitals are extremely popular as pedestals in the garden, on which to place statues, or other ornaments.

White marble balustrade
20 feet 6 inches long

Reputedly removed from Easton Neston, Northamptonshire. The formal gardens were originally laid out in the late 17th century when the house was built by Hawksmoor, perhaps with some collaboration from Wren, and restored by Sir Thomas Fermor Hesketh at the turn of the 19th century, when it is possible that the balustrade was installed.

Japanese carved stone lantern
220 cm. 106 in. high

Japanese lanterns are usually relatively simple in form and carved in granite. With its elaborate carving this is very much an exception, and its size makes it an impressive piece.

Victorian veined marble font
102 cm. 40 in. high

Removed from Chelmsford Cathedral, this makes a container for plants in the garden.

Wirework aviary
287 cm. 113 in. high

Of fairly basic design, the proportions nevertheless are pleasing to the eye; the only decoration is the overscrolling terminals on the roof. This 19th-century example is larger than most, since it is possible to walk into it.

Japanese bronze gateway
285 cm. 112 in. high

The simple lines of this gate inspire tranquillity and peace. Over the years the bronze has oxidized to give a mottled green patination. It would originally have stood at the entrance to a temple.

Selection of lead hoppers
the largest 54 cm. 21 in. high

Many large houses in the 17th and 18th centuries incorporated a lead guttering

system, which often bore the date that the house was built, and the initials of the owner. Later lead was often replaced by cast iron. Lead hoppers have subsequently proved popular for hanging on the walls of houses and gardens and planting out, in which role they look most effective.

Indian aviary of painted wood
240 cm. 94½ in. high

Originally conceived as an architectural canopy, this brightly painted structure has proved ideal for conversion into an aviary.

Wooden and lead flashed dome
432 cm. 170 in.

One of a pair, this originally surmounted a Victorian hospital. It would, however, translate very well into a garden, either simply as a folly, or possibly converted into a dovecote.

Victorian cast iron lamp post
254 cm. 100 in. high

The vast majority of 19th-century lamp posts, originally made for gas and later converted to electricity, are large and relatively plain since they were used in streets and public places. Smaller, more ornate examples such as this, are rarer and more popular. This would originally have stood on a parapet or wall and is missing the glazed copper lantern on the top.

Water and fountains

Lead fountain with a putto astride a stylized fish
66 cm. 26 in. high

Like most decorative leadwork this piece was produced earlier this century. The concept of the boy and fish with water issuing from the fish's mouth is a common one, to be found in a variety of forms and materials.

Lead fountain
155 cm. 57 in. high

A popular model still being produced by lead foundries today. A virtually identical design exists in the 1875 Coalbrookdale catalogue and it is likely that this copy was made from a mould taken from a cast iron example. Many lead fountains have suffered damage due to the malleable nature of the material, although lead does have an advantage over cast iron in not being susceptible to rust.

Coalbrookdale cast iron fountain
140 cm. 55 in. high

Coalbrookdale produced a number of fountains in this style using a number of interchangeable components, often with the same base, which also occurs in later copies in lead. This model, incorporating a Nubian maiden in the centre section, is one of the rarer examples.

Italianate Renaissance style bronze wellhead
c.1870, 272 cm. 107 in. high

An impressive and unusual piece. The bucket is suspended from the lion's mouth on a pulley system, while at the back of the wellhead is a fountain mask above a scallop shell bowl. Designed to be viewed in the round, perhaps in the centre of a courtyard, this makes the drawing of water infinitely more interesting than merely turning on a tap.

Cast iron fountain
198 cm. 78 in. high

Produced by the Handyside Foundry in Derby. The scallop shell bowl is particularly well modelled, with the often used motif of intertwined stylized dolphins and rockwork

base; the two putti above, however, appear too small and out of scale. The charm of this model is the water cascading over the scallop shell which meets plumes of water from the dolphins' nostrils.

Bronzed fountain of a baby
76 cm. 30 in. high

Produced this century, the core of this piece is plaster, with a coating of copper applied with electrolysis. It is an unusual concept for a fountain: the water is ejected in a fairly high pressure jet from the toad's mouth splashing directly into the child's face, which justifies his grimacing expression and flailing arms and legs!

Bronze fountain of a naked girl holding an umbrella
127 cm. 50 in. high

Sculpted in 1986 by Barbara Stride. The water spouts from the ferrule of the umbrella over the edges and onto the girl's outstretched hand. The idea is extremely effective, although one is tempted to wonder why a girl without clothes should want to shelter under an umbrella!

Spelter fountain group
90 cm. 35½ in. high

Spelter is a zinc based alloy, and is generally looked on as the poor relation of bronze. Invented in the middle of the last century it was extensively used for small statues and souvenirs. Although much softer than bronze or cast iron it does have the advantage of not being as susceptible to rust or oxidization. The mouths of the two dolphins are plumbed for water and the base is stamped J.W. Fiske, 99 Chambers St., New York. The softness of the material is evident in the cracking around the base.

Bronze fountain
145 cm. 58 in. high

A contemporary piece produced in Thailand, but very much in a Western style. Recent years have seen a proliferation of bronze foundries in Thailand where operating costs are a fraction of those in Europe and America. A number of models, including animals, fountains and figures, are being produced to European designs. Although not of the same quality as most 19th-century European bronzes, their standards are improving, especially in the different patinations which can be achieved. In this instance, what appears to be a weathered green patination has been achieved overnight by chemical means.

Bronze fountain
c.1880 122 cm. 48 in. high

The satyr's mouth and the beaks of the ducks he is holding are all plumbed for water – an unusual idea, since satyrs are not usually associated with either water or ducks; the whole group is rather uncomfortable both in its conception and execution of modelling.

Bronze bird bath
91 cm. 36 in. high

A rather athletic figure of Narcissus gazing at his reflection in the pool below, modelled by Eugène Désiré Piron late in the last century. The surface of the bronze has oxidized to produce a green patination, with whitish streaks thanks to the attentions of the local bird population.

Bronze fountain figure
56 cm. 22 in. high

The original, known as 'Mercury in Repose' and now in the Naples Museum, was discovered in Herculaneum in 1759, and is believed to be by the Hellenistic sculptor Lysippes, who lived at the court of Alexander the Great. Reproductions were extensively produced in the last century. The Chiurazzi foundry in Naples retailed this facsimile for 1,500 lire in 1929.

White marble fountain
193 cm. 76 in. high

Carved by Camille Gresland and dated 1907. The style, the naked woman with her wanton expression, and the pose are very much in the 20th-century idiom. There are two smaller pools behind and the water flows from small apertures flanking the devil's mask. The figure is carved in pure white statuary marble from Carrera whilst the pools are in a greyer veined marble.

Rosso Verona marble wellhead
91 cm. 36 in. high

Based on earlier Venetian designs with masks and armorials, examples such as this were produced at the end of the last century in Italy and were sold through firms such as J.P. White of Bedford, England. The originals would have incorporated a wrought iron overthrow supporting the pulley system and bucket. The 19th- and 20th-century copiers often even went to the trouble of filing grooves on the lip of the wellhead simulating the places where the ropes pulling up the bucket rubbed on the sides.

Rosso Verona marble bath
180 cm. 71 in. wide

Although carved at the end of the last century, the decoration is in the style of a 16th/17th-century Venetian wellhead. The bottom of the bath is stepped and has a drainage hole. Very few of these are now used as actual baths, since their enormous weight precludes them from being installed in most houses.

White marble bath
188 cm. 74 in. high

More usually now seen planted in gardens than in use as baths. Most examples have ring handles and are raised on paw feet. This has the addition of a well carved lion's mask.

Italian white marble fountain
c.1870, 178 cm. 70 in. high

A magnificent example which sadly bears no signature. Although a number of figures are incorporated into this piece, it does not appear over-fussy, since the overall symmetry is well balanced. The water is emitted from the bird's beak and the putto's conch shell. The rockwork base is deliberately stepped to be placed over the edge of a pool, creating an effective reflection when the fountains are not operating.

Marble fountain figure of Venus
208 cm. 82 in. high

Known as a 'trickle fountain', since the water merely trickles out at the top of the scallop shell, this 18th-century classical figure based on an antique prototype was meant to stand in a large pool, so that the water could flow over the edge of the bowl into the pool below.

Marble figure of a man supporting a birdbath
140 cm. 55 in. high

Produced in a pinkish grey marble in Italy this century, this piece has very little to commend it. The tattered clothes and hang-dog expression of the man present a very dismal image, while its large scale and weight precludes it from inclusion in most gardens.

Carved stone fountain
135 cm. 53 in. high

Carved in Italy in the 20th century of soft limestone from Vicenza, fountains of this manageable size and proportion have proved very popular. The softness of the stone means that it will weather very quickly; this process cannot be stopped, resulting, especially with fountains which are always wet, in eventual frost damage and subsequent crumbling of the stone.

White marble fountain
c.1900, 325 cm. 128 in. high

Carved in the form of a grotto to be set into a wall. The water, rather than being emitted in jets, runs down the front and is collected in the scallop shaped bowl. The white marble glistening with water highlights the grotto effect. The sculptor has successfully overcome the problems of carving in high relief and although there are no fewer than six figures in this piece, the maiden at the top with her lithe elongated body, so typical of this period, is perfectly poised with an outstretched arm and leg.

Venetian fountain bowl on stand
137 cm. 54 in. high

This curious arrangement has been made up of 18th-century Istrian stone components. The bowl, with its Venetian Byzantine influences, sits on the plain column with an armorial shield; the lower section is made up of two separate bases of differently coloured stone, mortared together. Despite this it remains a charming piece of useful size.

Large white statuary marble fountain
247 cm. 97 in. high

Although not signed this was probably produced in France at the end of the 19th century and combines a number of styles. The naked water nymph's fin-de-siècle features contrast with the Florentine-style grotesque mask spouting water flanked by stylised dolphins. It is not conceived as a piece to be viewed in the round since the back is plain, but the balance of her overhanging leg is perfectly counterpointed by her outstretched elbow as she gazes, Narcissus like, at her reflection in the pool below.

White marble fountain
71 cm. 28 in. high

A traditional approach for a fountain, often associated with the Florentine Renaissance, produced in Italy c.1880. The boy astride the dolphin on a wave-carved base has been produced in a number of media.

Italian white marble fountain
94 cm. 37 in. high

Made in the last century, this example is crisply carved with a variety of foliate motifs, and with dolphins on the corners of the base. The inside of the bowl is carved in relief with swimming fish and eels, an amusing conceit reminiscent of the similarly decorated oriental porcelain fish bowls in blue and white and polychrome.

Rosso Verona marble bath
96 cm. 38 in. high

The basin was retailed in England at the end of the last century, complete with spurious armorial shield, and until recently was positioned next to a swimming pool as a foot bath. The lead figure of the putto was added later. It would be more effective if the figure had been plumbed for water, making it a fountain of manageable proportions.

Stone wellhead
279 cm. 110 in. diameter

Of Continental origin. The decoration, apart from the wrought iron overthrow, is very plain, unlike the smaller Venetian examples. It is probable that this originally stood in a public place such as a town square.

Composition stone fountain base
127 cm. 50 in. high

Although made of artificial stone produced in a mould this example has over the years attracted a wonderful weathered patina. A fountain figure would originally have stood on the top; the mouths of the lion masks on all four sides are plumbed for water.

Composition stone fountain
230 cm. 90 in. high

Manufactured in Italy in moulds using an aggregate including marble dust and chips. The various components are interchangeable, and similar pieces can still be purchased today.

Stoneware birdbath
114 cm. 45 in. high

Although not stamped, this is very much in the style of Doulton pieces produced at the end of the last century. It has unfortunately been painted, which obscures the original buff colour of the clay. It is often extremely difficult to strip pieces in this condition, since even though relatively non-porous, the material does absorb some of the paint.

Coade stone grotto fountain
135 cm. 53 in. high, stamped Coade and Sealy Lambeth and dated 1805

The forerunner of the more well-known 19th-century artificial stoneware factories such as Doulton, the Coade factory was remarkable in being established by a woman, Mrs Eleanor Coade, in 1769. The basic ingredient was grog-stoneware clay which was fired in a kiln, ground up and fired in moulds, producing a very durable product with fine detail. The coral work ingeniously incorporating animal masks and stalactites below harks back to the 18th-century interest in grottos. John Sealy was in partnership with Eleanor Coade between 1799 and his death in 1813.

Doulton stoneware fountain
15 in. diameter

Produced in the 1890s; Doulton produced a number of garden fountains and ornaments between about 1860 and 1910. John Broad, Pope, and George Tinworth were the leading exponents in this style, and the more architectural effects of Tinworth's work would suggest that he was responsible for modelling this piece. Stoneware, which is fired to a high temperature in a kiln, is impervious to water, a very necessary attribute in garden pieces to prevent frost damage.

Statuary

Lead figure of Cupid
94 cm. 37 in. high

Produced earlier this century after an original by the Danish sculptor Bertal Thorwaldsen, who was living and working in Rome from 1797 to 1838, very much in the classical tradition. The patination of this piece and the modelling would suggest that it is older than it really is, especially since much of the decorative leadwork produced this century takes its inspiration from earlier styles.

Lead figure of Punch, 18th century
112 cm. 44 in. high

The origins of Punch are lost in the Italian Middle Ages, but he was as popular in the 18th century as he is today. The sculptor has accentuated his deformities by lengthening his arms and shortening his legs. The modelling and detail in his leering expression and flowing hair is of the highest

quality, making this a very rare and desirable figure. Like other 18th-century lead figures he has suffered damage on his leg where the rusting iron support rod has expanded. It is possible that this piece was modelled by John Cheere who took over John van Nost's lead yard around 1739. J.T. Smith in *Streets of London* gives the following description of Cheere's yard – 'The figures were cast in lead as large as life and frequently painted with the intention to resemble nature. They consisted of Punch, Harlequin, Columbine and other Pantomime characters.' As a rough pointer for deciding whether a lead figure belongs to the 18th or late 19th/20th century, it is worth noting that the vast majority of 18th-century lead figures are fixed to stone bases, while later examples have integral lead bases. Very little leadwork was produced during the 19th century; it went out of fashion in the face of competition from cast iron which could be more cheaply mass-produced, and only returned to favour during the last years of the 19th century.

Pair of lead putti, each on Portland stone base
85 cm. 33½ in. high

These 18th-century examples demonstrate very well the difference between leadwork of this period and that of the 19th and 20th centuries. Cast with the *cire perdu*, or lost wax, process more commonly associated with bronzes, it could achieve far greater detail than slush or sand castings used later. The sculptor has demonstrated his technical skill by standing each putto on only one leg. Unfortunately this will ultimately lead to their literal downfall, since it involved an iron rod being placed through the supporting leg, packed with clay and then fitted into a hole in the stone base which was then filled with molten lead. Over the years moisture often gets into the supporting leg and rusts the iron rod which then expands, splitting the leg. Many were badly and unsympathetically repaired by estate plumbers, and the rarity of 18th-century lead statues is partially explained by this. Others were melted down.

Pair of lead figures of a shepherd and shepherdess
125 cm. 49 in. high

These are copies of 18th-century originals modelled by John Cheere and possibly mentioned in *Leaves in a Manuscript Diary* (London 1772) in which Cheere's yard is described thus: 'Mr Cheere's yard, which, on account of numerous figures in stone, lead and plaster, you would swear was a country fair or market, made up of spruce squires, haymakers with rakes in their hands, shepherds and shepherdesses.' These later copies lack the detail and quality of their 18th-century counterparts but still have traces of paint. It is interesting to note that they have integral lead bases.

Two lead figures representing Spring and Summer
102 cm. 40 in. high

Produced by J.P. White of Bedford early this century, these are amongst the best modelled of a large range of lead figures of seasons belonging to his period. They both are standing next to tree stumps; this strengthens them, since many lead figures tend to break at the ankles, the weakest point of the construction.

Lead figure of a putto
81 cm. 32 in. high
Lead figure of a young girl
94 cm. 37 in. high

Both figures are well modelled and balanced; the swirling drapery over the young girl's head is particularly effective. Firms such as H. Crowther & Son of Chiswick, and a relatively new firm, the Bulbeck Foundry of Burwell, Cambridgeshire, are still producing a variety of such pieces.

Lead figure of a blackamoor
117 cm. 46 in. high

A similar blackamoor and Indian were originally made for Hampton Court by John van Nost the elder in 1701. They were perhaps originally intended as part of a larger set representing all the continents, but William III died two months after the erection of the first two. Like many 18th-century lead figures, this one's leg has been split by the rusting of the iron core. The feather skirt still shows traces of early paint, since many 18th-century lead figures were painted in naturalistic colours.

Pair of lead dogs
53 cm. 21 in. high

Very much in the style of Joseph Gott, 1786-1860, the English sculptor who specialized in carving greyhounds and whippets in white marble. These examples are in lead and date from the 20th century, but they succeed in recapturing the mood and movement of their predecessors in the quality of the modelling.

English 18th-century lead figure of Spring
152 cm. 60 in. high, on panelled pedestal

This figure is derived from an original marble work by the French sculptor Laurent Magnier (1615-1700). The design for Magnier's Spring (which was executed between 1674 and 1681) was supplied, together with designs for three companion seasons, by Charles Le Brun (1619-1690). All four original marble works remain today in the gardens at Versailles. This lead statue, like a number of 18th-century lead figures, is in fact a reversed copy of its original, and so must have been modelled from a print. A possible source of the original print is *Figures, Groupes, Thermes, Fontaines, Vases et Autres Ornemens ... dans le Chateau et Parc de Versailles,* which not only illustrates Magnier's Spring (see illustration) but also the three companion seasons from designs by Le Brun:

the Summer executed by Pierre Hutinot (1616-1679)
the Autumn executed by Thomas Regnaudin (1622-1706)
the Winter executed by François Girardon (1628-1715)

Similarly reversed and slightly modified examples of Hutinot's Summer and Girardon's Winter, by the eminent 18th-century lead figure maker John Cheere (1709-1787), survive in the gardens at Southill.

Like many 18th-century lead pieces, this example has over the years been painted many times, which has obscured a lot of the original fine detail.

Pair of lead gate pier finials cast in the form of satyrs
73 cm. 29 in. high

A quite charming example of late 19th-century lead work which, in quality, almost bears comparison with pieces produced in the 18th century.

Pair of cast iron figures of pages
226 cm. 89 in. high

Although signed E. Houssin and bearing the date 1882, these are contemporary copies produced by the Salin foundry in France. Attractive in subject matter, they are well cast and bear witness to the still underrated tradition of 19th-century French figurative cast iron.

One of a pair of cast iron lions
102 cm. 40 in. long

This and similar animal groups were extensively produced by American foundries which had formerly been producing munitions for the American Civil War. The subsequent decline in the need for cannon forced many to diversify their interests into producing a variety of cast iron wares including decorative railings and architectural fittings, garden ornaments and even the well known cast iron piggy banks.

Pair of cast iron figures of a lion and tiger
145 cm. 57 in. high

A pair of figures modelled by Alfred Jacquemart, cast at the Val d'Osne Foundry and illustrated in their trade catalogue (see

illustration). Pieces in bronze have always been commercially more desirable than those in cast iron and this pair of animals would command a price perhaps five times higher in bronze.

Pair of cast iron figures of a wolf and boar
79 cm. 31 in. high

Modelled by Alfred Jacquemart and stamped 'A.J.' and with founder's plaque inscribed 'Founderies de Val d'Osne Rue Voltaire Paris.' Alfred Jacquemart, 1824-1896, was one of a number of 19th-century French *animalier* sculptors mainly working on a small scale in bronze. He did, however, produce a number of life-size models in cast iron founded by the Val d'Osne and Durenne foundries. This pair were probably originally commissioned to go on the gate piers of a substantial French hunting lodge.

One of a pair of alloy lions
102 cm. 40 in. high

Impressive in their size, these probably formed part of a municipal monument in France earlier this century. The quality of the modelling is very fine, especially the way in which the paws and tail overhang the edge of the base, a technique often used in the 18th century.

Pair of Japanese bronze cranes
130 cm. 31 in. high

The use of animal bronzes in Japanese gardens has a long history. Most of the animals have symbolic meaning, the cranes representing longevity. They were often placed at the edge of shallow ponds; sometimes the integral bases are cast with naturalistic plants such as lily leaves, and even crabs and other small aquatic fauna. They are usually constructed in a number of pieces; the necks and legs are usually made separately and fixed together with small bolts. Modern copies from Thailand tend to be in one piece.

One of a pair of Japanese bronze toads
24 cm. 9½ in. high

Toads are credited in Japanese mythology with magic powers but bronze ones are rarer than cranes. These have acquired beautiful green patination, which when wet makes their naturalistically cast wart-covered bodies deceptively life-like.

Coalbrookdale cast iron figure of a water putto
81 cm. 31 in. high

A quite charming example of Coalbrookdale's work on a modest scale.

Cast iron tethering post
102 cm. 40 in. high

Modelled as a jockey in silks. This would have been produced by an American foundry c. 1870. The face and hands have been painted dark, though the modelling of the face and hair are not negroid.

Bronze figure of a girl
signed Johann Eduard Muller and dated 1877, 180 cm. 70 in. high

This rare life-size piece is entitled 'Ecco il Moccola' which means literally 'Here is the light'. The girl is holding aloft a short length of electric cable extolling the recently discovered virtues of electricity.

Bronze figure of Mercury
183 cm. 72 in. high

After a well-known original by the Italian Renaissance sculptor Giambologna, this is one of the most reproduced examples of Italian art, and can be seen in a variety of materials and sizes, many of which were brought to England during the last century. This piece, which is larger than most, has lost the caduceus, a snake-entwined wand, which Mercury holds in his left hand.

Cast iron figure of a maiden
155 cm. 61 in. high

Produced by the Durenne Foundry at Someville c. 1860 in the Egyptian taste. These figures supporting a light were intended for both indoor use in hallways or on the newel posts of imposing staircases, or else flanking steps outside a house.

White marble group of an Amazon on horseback
90 cm. 35½ in. high on veined marble pedestal, 114 cm. 45 in. high

The original life-size bronze executed by Professor Kiss in Berlin and entitled 'Amazon being attacked by a panther' was first exhibited in 1862, after which a number of copies were made. It is an immensely powerful image in which the panther's claws can be seen ripping into the horse's flesh, though its appeal is limited since the subject matter is distasteful to many people. The quality of the pedestal is especially worthy of comment; not many come onto the market and they sometimes fetch higher prices than the sculpture placed on them.

Pair of white marble hoppocampi
86 cm. 34 in. high

Beautifully modelled and crisply carved, these magnificent mythological beasts with their wave carved bases would originally have flanked a pool of some sort.

Italian white marble figure of a vestal virgin
117 cm. 46 in. high

Carved in the late 18th/early 19th century, this piece is very successful in the modelling of the intricate robes, but the overall image is nevertheless rather unexciting.

Italian white marble figure of Ruth
125 cm. 49 in. high

Religious pieces are not popular as garden ornaments, but this statue of Ruth drawing water at the well is charming enough to overcome such a prejudice. The sculptor, unfortunately unknown since the piece is unsigned, has very successfully conveyed the various textures of her smooth skin, her dress, the rope and the wall of the well.

One of a set of four marble busts of maidens representing the seasons
each signed A. Bottinelli F. Roma.
105 cm. 73 in. high

Busts on pedestals have always proved popular in gardens, to flank paths or to stand in niches created in hedges. This set of four,

dating from c. 1870, are slightly weathered through being out of doors. The top of each pedestal incorporates an iron framed turntable which, over the years, has rusted, producing yellowy brown discolouration. Unfortunately rust marks are almost impossible to get out of marble short of actually grinding them out.

Pair of white marble figures of Cupid and Psyche
signed G.M. Benzoni and dated 1863
117 cm. 46 in. high on pedestals

Giovanni Maria Benzoni, 1809-1873, was a prolific sculptor working in Rome. It is a matter of conjecture whether pieces such as this were intended for outdoor use. The great Italian palazzi with interior courtyards surrounded with a loggia quite often housed marble sculptures in niches, which although outside, were at least under cover. But sculpture brought back by gentlemen on the Grand Tour of Europe was often consigned to the garden, since apart from the great English houses such as Petworth, Chatsworth or Wilton with their sculpture galleries, there was nowhere to put them under cover. White marble, in common with most other materials, is susceptible to the elements. The harsher weather and heavier rainfall of Northern Europe eventually leads to decay. The surface of the marble becomes abraded and 'sugary' in appearance, resulting in a gradual crumbling of the carved details. The 20th-century phenomenon of acid rain has further exacerbated this problem. There are, however, those who actually prefer marble sculpture in a slightly weathered condition, maintaining that muted mellow colours are more appropriate to the English countryside than the crisp whiteness that suits the hot climate of Italy.

White marble group of St Michael
signed J.G. Lough and dated 1870
262 cm. 103 in. high

John Graham Lough, 1798-1876, attracted both praise and ridicule by his work, which included a number of royal commissions. This rather uncomfortable figure looks as if the archangel is gently sliding off the globe. Both hands and feet have been replaced with badly carved copies.

White marble figure of a classical youth
122 cm. 48 in. high

Produced in the early part of the 19th century in Italy, this well modelled piece, although recently cleaned, has suffered the ravages of a Northern climate; his fingers and nose have become badly worn. Note that there are connecting pieces of marble between his arm and body and from his staff to his leg. These were left by the sculptor as strengthening members for shipping and were meant to be removed when it finally reached its destination. It is amusing to see how many similar pieces today still have these strengthening armatures 150 years after they should have been taken off.

White marble figure of a boy
86 cm. 34 in. high

This very charming late 19th-century portrait figure is unusual in its execution. The boy, holding a posy holder, and dressed in frock coat, jabot, breeches and silk stockings with buckled court shoes, may be portrayed in the finery of a page boy at a wedding.

White marble figure of a prophet
153 cm. 60 in. high

This 18th-century figure was designed specifically to be displayed outside and so is characterized by a lack of extravagent modelling. The understated folds of drapery ensure that no water can gather, eventually eroding the piece.

Set of three white marble figures of the Holy Family
The Christ Child 170 cm. 67 in. high

Well executed in pure white statuary marble at the end of the last century in Italy, and destined either for a church or graveyard. The subject matter rather than the quality is the deciding factor in making these relatively less popular in today's market.

White marble figure of a young boy plucking a thorn from his foot
61 cm. 24 in. high

After a famous antique bronze model known as the Spinaro, recorded as early as 1165 outside the Lateran Palace, Rome, and reproduced in a variety of materials. It was later noticed that the head on the original must, at some time, have been replaced since, as well as its being stylistically different, one would expect the boy's long hair to be hanging straight down since his head is bent over. The green serpentine marble pedestal is typical of a large number produced in the 19th century, often with rotating tops on which statues and busts could be placed both indoors and in gardens.

White marble figure of an Amazon
132 cm. 52 in. high

The Amazons were a mythical race of female warriors originating in Asia Minor and mentioned by several classical authors. This one, standing holding a bow, and with her helmet at her feet, is reasonably well modelled and carved, but would have been produced in Italy purely on a decorative level for an export market.

White marble figure of St Fiacre
166 cm. 65 in. high

St Fiacre, who died c.670, is the patron saint of horticulturists and as such is depicted here next to a bunch of gathered twigs, and holding a spade.

White marble figure
180 cm. 71 in. high

Signed Ant° Argenti Milano, this figure, carved about 1880, was originally an angel with wings and would have formed a rather impressive monument in a graveyard. The removal of the wings makes her more secular in appearance, but her mournful, downcast expression and the cross emblazoned on her robe, is still sufficient indication of her origins to give her only limited popular appeal.

One of a pair of white marble lions
150 cm. 60 in. high

Lions have always been a popular subject. These magnificent 19th-century Italian beasts supporting armorial shields, and with heads slightly inclined towards each other, would provide extremely imposing features crowning gate piers.

White marble group of a maiden and goat
Signed 'A. Bottinelli F. {Fecit} Roma' and titled 'Le Prime Rose'
135 cm. 53 in. high, on veined marble column pedestal 74 cm. 29 in. high

A well balanced group by Antonio Bottinelli c. 1870 in which the semi-naked girl is trying to prevent the goat, whose collar is hung with bells, from eating a bunch of roses held at her side. The pedestal emphasises the need for groups such as this to be raised up to eye level. On the ground the girl's face would be hidden, and much of the charm lost.

White marble bust of the dying Alexander
80 cm. 30½ in. high

A good quality late 17th/early 18th century bust after an antique model, first recorded as belonging to the Medici Family in Florence in 1597 when Giambologna was commissioned to fit it onto a statue. It has been in the Uffizi since at least the end of the 17th century, but this example differs from the Uffizi original since it incorporates a robe draped over one shoulder.

Large white marble copy of the Apollo Belvedere
228 cm. 90 in. high

With the advent of the Grand Tour in the 17th century the nobility and gentry of Britain and Northern Europe brought back, as visible evidence of their classical education, copies of the great sculpture produced in antiquity, which was still being discovered during the excavations in Italy. By the 19th century a large industry had developed centred around Rome, Florence and Naples to manufacture these copies, many of which still grace the gardens of Europe.

White marble group of the Three Graces
dated 1830, 114 cm. 45 in. high

A faithful and well carved copy of Canova's original carved earlier in the 19th century. Besides copying models after the antique, Italian sculptors also went to famous works of contemporaries such as Thorwaldsen and Canova.

White marble group of a bitch and puppy
87 cm. 34 in. high on plinth
99 cm. 39 in. high
Signed 'Francis Cucchiari' and carved c. 1840

This reproduces an antique original in the Muso Pio Clementino, Vatican. Dogs as a subject matter have always proved popular and this group, correctly raised at eye level on a plinth, effectively conveys the maternal instincts of the bitch as she protectively places her paw on the back of her puppy beneath her.

Large white marble group entitled 'Fleurs due Amavo'
signed 'F. Charpentier' and dated 1912, 230 cm. 90½ in. high

Felix Charpentier 1858-1924, studied under Cavelier at the École des Beaux Arts

and exhibited at the Salon from 1884 onwards, winning several medals. This piece, carved from a single massive block of marble and designed to be set into a wall, contrasts the sensuous qualities of the girl's body, and her inhaling the scent of a bouquet of flowers held to her face, with the roughly hewn amorphous mass of marble surrounding her. It ably demonstrates the sculptor's skill in interrelating different textures and forms since in this case one appears to grow out of the other.

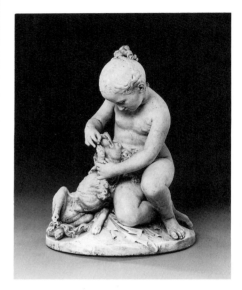

Pair of white marble groups signed 'G.M. Benzoni 1851 Roma'
71 cm. 28 in. high

A number of versions of these groups were produced by Giovanni Maria Benzoni, and the enormous size of his output would suggest that he employed a large workshop of assistants. In one group a young naked child lovingly plucks a thorn from the puppy's foot, while in the other, the now fully grown dog crushes a snake with his paw to save his mistress. The allegorical nature of these pieces is typical of the period.

White marble figure of Apollo
147 cm. 58 in. high

The carving of this early 19th-century piece borders on the naive. The head is too small for the body and the modelling of the drapery clumsy and without movement. Many similar pieces are still to be found in Spain and Portugal, lacking the sophistication of their Italian counterparts.

White marble group entitled Venere Amore and signed 'Biggi Fausto'
127 cm. 50 in. high

A typically Italian group dating to 1870, incorporating the classical elements of a winged Cupid and an inscription, combined with a sentimental treatment of Venus. The textures of the flesh contrasted with the rocky base and the overhanging fern fronds work particularly well.

One of a large pair of white marble dogs of Fo
155 cm. 61 in. high

These are modern pieces produced in the Far East and available in a number of sizes. Dogs of Fo in Chinese mythology are traditionally temple guardians. The male is depicted with one paw resting on a ball, while his mate rests hers on one of her young. The bases are carved with dragons chasing the flaming pearl – representing the striving for spiritual purity, one of the most popular representations in Chinese mythological art. In common with other spheres of production, the low labour costs in the Far East means that these can be produced extremely competitively.

White marble group entitled 'A Wood Nymph'
153 cm. 60 in. high

Inscribed on the base 'Executed for the Art Union of London by C.B. Birch Dec. 1,

1865'. This charming group by Charles Birch epitomizes Victorian sculpture. It has been extensively reproduced on a smaller scale in Parian ware.

Kilkenny marble statue of Cupid
130 cm. 51 in. high

Carved in Kilkenny marble, a very hard igneous stone. This figure reflects the affluence of the gentry of 18th-century Ireland. It is probably copied by a local immigrant sculptor from a late 17th-century engraving since, despite the difficulty of carving such a hard, brittle material, it shows a remarkable fluidity of movement. It has, over the years, lost an arm and is now covered with moss and lichen, which heightens its Arcadian appeal.

Venetian stone statue of Hercules
210 cm. 87 in. high

The lack of attention to close detail on this 18th-century figure and the mannerist exaggeration of the muscles would indicate that it was designed to stand perhaps 50 feet up in the air on the parapet of a Venetian palazzo, probably as one of a series.

Set of carved stone figures on pedestals representing the seasons
284 cm. 112 in. high

Carved in soft Vicenza stone perhaps in the 1970s, these are just beginning to acquire a slightly weathered look. Sadly this does not help the lack of quality in the modelling or the simpering stereotyped expressions on their faces. They are carved using mechanical tools rather than by hand, and can easily be identified by the regular panelled machine-gouged lines on the bases.

Late 18th- early 19th-century carved stone figure of a classical maiden
168 cm. 66 in. high

This figure, which is only partially finished at the back and has rebates on the stone base, would originally have sat on the parapet of a building, flanking a pediment, probably with a companion figure on the other side, since the composition flows diagonally from her legs up to her upraised arms.

Limestone figure of a soldier in armour, 18th-century
194 cm. 76 in. high

Now covered with moss and lichen, extensively damaged and with missing limbs, which in some ways enhances its appeal, this figure would look perfect in an Arcadian garden setting.

Neo-Gothic sandstone figure of a king
early 19th century, 145 cm. 57 in. high

This sandstone figure removed from the Palace of Westminster most probably dates from the Gothic Revival work of Wyatt on the Houses of Parliament around 1805 and was presumably removed at the time of the fire of 1834 and the subsequent rebuilding by Sir Charles Barry. It is a good example of a piece of architectural embellishment which has translated well into the garden.

Pair of 18th-century Portland stone dogs
95 cm. 27 in. high

Carved in Portland stone — a hard light-coloured stone much favoured in the 18th century — these superb examples would originally have stood on gate piers.

Two carved stone groups representing Hunting and Fishing by Falconet and dated 1780
183 cm. 72 in. high

Etienne Maurice Falconet, 1716-1791, was one of the most brilliant sculptors of his day. The composition of these two groups is identical to those in Sèvres biscuit porcelain modelled by Falconet in 1758 for Louis XV. Both groups are designed to be seen in the round; both are carved with two maidens and putto, with either a dead deer and hunting dog or fish being hauled in a net. The composition is masterful, as is the quality of carving, but the softness of the stone has resulted in a lot of the surface detail flaking off. This process can only be arrested by either putting the groups indoors or embarking on a lengthy, skilled, and extremely expensive restoration programme.

One of a pair of composition stone lions
97 cm. 38 in. high

Cast from moulds in the mid-20th century, these show what can be achieved using composition stone. They are well modelled and in their relatively short life have achieved a beautiful patination of moss and lichen which makes them more desirable than their age or mass-produced provenance would suggest.

Plaster bust of Georges Cuvier after David d'Angers
76 cm. 38 in.

Inscribed 'A la Memoire de Georges Cuvier David d'Angers, 1838.' Pierre Jean David, 1788-1856, better known as David d'Angers, where he was born, bridged the gap between classicism and Romanticism in the last century. Plaster copies would have been produced in large quantities but the nature of the material does not make it suitable for the garden on a long-term basis.

Composition figure of a classical maiden
20th century, 218 cm. 86 in. high, on pedestal

Composition stone (as opposed to artificial stone an 18th-century term where the clay product is fired in a kiln) has been in existence far longer than is generally realised. It is usually largely composed of sand and cement, sometimes with an aggregate of crushed stone added, and is sometimes rather grandly referred to as *ciment fondue*. Most of the composition stone seen today was produced this century. The attraction of such pieces is the weathering which they have acquired over the years. Just as on a piece of antique furniture a patina of dust, polish and handling is achieved over a long period of time, so a composition stone piece will gather moss, lichen and dirt. There are a number of additives, such as soot and yoghurt, which will accelerate this effect.

Coade stone sphinx
122 cm. 48 in high

Produced shortly before the Coade factory ceased production in 1843, when the moulds were sold.

Pair of Doulton stoneware figures of maidens representing Spring and Summer
114 cm. 45 in. high

Originally conceived as a set of four figures of the Seasons, these are quite rare, since most of the garden pieces produced by Doulton at the end of the last century were non-figurative.

One of a pair of carved wooden stags
214 cm. 84 in. high

Of Balinese origin and carved in hardwood, these are quite resilient to the elements, and in the right setting, look impressive. The backs have been hollowed out to accommodate planters.

Urns and vases

Lidded urn
20th century, 84 cm. 33 in. high

A good example of how eclecticism of design can go badly wrong. The body is cast with 17th-century style amorini, but the overall shape owes more to the 1930s, clashing to produce a piece without much aesthetic merit. The two planters flanking it are based on 17th-century water cisterns, though on a smaller, more manageable scale, the one on the left bearing the entirely bogus date of 1689.

One of a pair of 20th-century lead urns
75 cm. 29½ in. high

Modelled on the Adam style. This classic form is often seen in the decoration of the late 18th century, but examples are still being produced by lead foundries today.

One of a pair of lead urns in the late 17th-century style
50 cm. 23 in. high

The bodies are cast with puffy cheeked putti, a popular motif of the time. The gadrooning at the foot follows the style adopted in silver of the period.

Lead urn
76 cm. 30 in. high

Produced at the end of the last century but copying Renaissance examples at Hampton Court, England. The quality of chasing and finishing is better than average, producing crisp detailing, although the modelling and herm handles leave a lot to be desired.

One of a pair of lead urns
96 cm. 38 in. high

The long cylindrical proportions make it look rather uncomfortable. This pair are cast with the date 1898 and a coat of arms, suggesting that they were individually commissioned for a particular house. Dating and armorials of this kind are more often seen on lead or cast iron hoppers, incorporated into the guttering of houses of the period.

One of a pair of lead urns
86 cm. 34 in. high

Probably produced on the Continent, and of a thicker gauge metal to prevent the foot becoming crushed over the years. The decoration is considerably crisper than average.

Pair of lead lidded urns
96 cm. 38 in. high

Probably produced by the Bromsgrove Guild in Worcestershire at the turn of the century, best known for executing the gates and railings at Buckingham Palace. These urns were made to crown gate piers. They were designed to be seen from below, where the top-heavy proportions of a swell foot and overhanging lid would appear to be in perspective.

Lead urn
38 cm. 15 in. high

Produced at the beginning of this century, but very much in the 17th-century style, with herm handles and amorini decoration. The inherent softness of the metal has meant that many examples, including this one, have buckled at the foot, crushed by its own weight.

One of a pair of cast iron urns
56 cm. 22 in. high

Although standard in design, these have been cast with sloping square bases, to be placed on top of gate piers.

One of a pair of cast iron urns on stands
104 cm. 40 in. high

Instead of being simply fluted and lobed, these 19th-century examples, with their grotesque head handles and scrolling cartouches of flowering cornucopia, display the elaborate overfussiness typical of Victorian design in so many fields.

Large cast iron urn on stand
280 cm. 110 in. high

Although not stamped, this impressive example was produced by the Ducel et Fils Foundry in the Pas-de-Calais in the second half of the last century. Its sheer size makes it an ideal centrepiece for a garden or a feature to be placed at the end of a vista. Urns of this size are relatively rare, although its size and grandeur preclude its use in the average garden.

Cast iron urn
82 cm. 32 in. high

Produced by the Val d'Osne Foundry in the Haute Marne region of France. A direct copy of one of a pair of bronze vases designed by Claude Ballin for Louis XIV at Versailles.

One of a pair of cast iron urns or flower stands
102 cm. 42 in. high

Produced in the second half of the last century. Over the years it has been given many coats of paint which have obscured much of the friezes of scrolling foliage, resulting in a rather woolly lumpy appearance.

One of a pair of cast iron urns
58 in./23 in. high on pedestals

An identical design is described in the Coalbrookdale catalogue rather fancifully as the 'Naples' pattern. Many of the same basic elements of design recur over and over again in the urns produced in the last century: the same semi-lobed body, egg-and-dart moulded rim and fluted rising circular foot.

239

Cast iron urn
107 cm. 42 in. high

Urns of this type were specifically designed for planting, and similar designs in the Coalbrookdale and Handyside catalogues of the last century describe them as 'flower stands.' The bowl is typical of the form more usually seen as a shallow lobed urn on a rising fluted circular foot and square base.

Cast iron urn
82 cm. 32 in. high

The style is associated with Thomas Hope, the influential English designer responsible for much of the neo-classical taste in the early 19th century. However, although unmarked, this urn undoubtedly originated from France, possibly copying an antique urn, since an identical design occurs in the Barbezat & Cie catalogue of the mid 1860s while nothing exactly like it can be found in Hope's *Household Furniture and Interior Decoration* published in 1807.

Cast iron urn
78 cm. 31½ in. high

One of the most popular patterns, produced in very large quantities throughout the 19th and 20th centuries in a variety of materials, with a semi lobed and fluted body and egg-and-dart moulded rim. Examples can be found in all sizes, ranging from small ones destined for a conservatory, to much larger examples used on terraces, flanking steps, or singly as centrepieces.

One of a pair of bronze urns
84 cm. 33 in. high

These bronze urns are copies of originals believed to have been cast by Duval from designs by Louis XIV's goldsmith Claude Ballin, which remain today on short marble plinths separating the Parterre du Nord from the Parterre d'Eau at Versailles. They possibly originate from Bagatelle in the Bois de Boulogne, the estate of the fourth Marquess of Hertford, 1800-1860, who through his friendship with Napoleon III was allowed to make bronze copies of the originals. On the death of the Marquess in 1870 the estate passed to his son, Sir Richard Wallace, and subsequently, on his death, to his secretary Sir John Murray, who removed all the urns except three pairs to England, selling the estate to the City of Paris in 1904.

Cast iron urn
41 cm. 16 in. high

A common classical design that combines the shallow lobed urn and foliate upswept handles. This is most probably French in manufacture.

One of a set of four cast iron urns
61 cm. 24 in. high

Another classical variation on the campana shape, this time with a frieze of scrolling foliage, and mask and loop handles. This set is rare in being stamped by the maker, A. Handyside & Co. of London & Derby. Unlike other cast iron garden furniture, very few urns bear makers' names, probably because they were so common and so similar.

Mid 18th-century white marble urn
150 cm. 59 in. high

Many of these monumental urns with ram's handles, originating from Italy, are still to be found in the gardens of French châteaux. This example has weathered well so that the garish whiteness of the marble has been toned down, but the nature of the material is still discernible.

White marble urn
183 cm. 72 in. high

Moulded with a frieze of anthemion and acanthus c. 1840. This again is a variation on the campana design, with the addition of loop handles and frieze of scrolling acanthus.

One of a pair of white marble urns
56 cm. 22 in. high

Of Indian origin, and to Western eyes perhaps not very pleasing in its proportions. Indian marble tends to be more crystalline than Italian; the flowerheads are typically Indian in design.

Shallow lobed marble urn
98 cm. 38½ in. diameter

A very common 19th-century model. A number originally stood in the large gardens surrounding Crystal Palace.

White marble urn
50 cm. 20 in. high

Of usual semi-lobed campana form produced in large quantities in Italy, and either brought back by people on the Grand Tour, or else retailed by firms such as Pearson Page

of Birmingham, and J. P. White of Bedford, from whose lavishly illustrated catalogues at the end of the last century urns in a variety of styles and materials could be purchased.

Early 19th-century stone urn
152 cm. 60 in. high

Sadly the softness of the stone has resulted in considerable weathering and damage. The mask and loop handles have been broken and the detail worn flat. However it does give these period pieces a slightly Arcadian air redolent of decaying splendour and in the right setting these drawbacks can be an advantage.

Polished pink granite urn
120 cm. 47 in. high

Probably produced by a local stonemason, and rather clumsy in its proportions. Polished granite has a very hard surface which is not susceptible to weathering, so that many pieces, even though of some age, continue to look new. It is sad that it has been used so extensively in graveyards. Stone, like people, should be allowed to grow old gracefully.

Louis XV stone finial
180 cm. 71 in. high

Probably originally intended to adorn the parapet or roof of a château. Despite being in a weathered condition, it is evident that the carving has never been of a high quality, suggesting that they were not made to be viewed from close to.

Pair of stone urns on pedestals
100 cm. 39 in. high

Carved in a fairly soft stone earlier this century, these pieces are still very crisp in detail. They are still fairly new and will benefit from weathering over the years.

Istrian stone trough
203 cm. 80 in. wide

This late 19th-century piece is carved with a quasi-armorial shield and fruiting vines and has channels and a drainage hole inside, fancifully suggesting that it is a wine press. It is unlikely that any grapes have ever been trodden in it, but it makes a very suitable planting trough for the garden.

One of a pair of Italian stone finials
68 cm. 27 in. high

Indigenous to the Vicenza region of Italy, the soft limestone takes on a weathered look remarkably quickly. Carved this century; the flat tops look as if they need some sort of lid to make them more pleasing to the eye.

Stone planter
53 cm. 21 in. high

Another piece in the range of 20th-century Italian wares carved in soft limestone from Vicenza. Because of its softness the stone has weathered quickly.

One of a pair of 19th-century Portland stone urns
Approximately 190 cm. 75 in. high

Quite a grand pair of urns of substantial size. They were made in sections, so that components can easily get lost or even mixed up with other pieces. The pineapple finial on this example has been replaced at some period, since it is considerably lighter in colour; no doubt it weathered more than other parts of the urn.

Pair of early 18th-century lidded urns attributed to Jan Pieter van Baurscheit the Elder
130 cm. 51 in. high

Baurscheit, a well-known sculptor of the time, has used the urn as a vehicle for his talents; each side of each urn is carved in relief with a scene from classical mythology, no easy task given the constraints of space. Each vignette can be appreciated for itself without detracting from the overall symmetry and proportions of the urns. Similar urns can be seen in the Rijksmuseum, Amsterdam; Waddesdon Manor, Buckinghamshire; and Panshanger, Hertfordshire, signed and dated 1714.

Portland stone urn, 18th-century
70 cm. 27½ in. high

Sadly this example has lost its foot. The body of the urn conforms to a more or less standard pattern with lobing beneath fruiting swags, but the addition of further fruit and sheaves of corn sprouting out of the top is an unusual bonus.

Composition stone urn
155 cm. 61 in. diameter

Although of a very standard pattern, the impressive size and diameter of this urn makes it a rare piece. It is difficult to date, since composition stone – an aggregate usually of sand and cement – has been in production since the early years of the 19th century.

Composition stone urn on pedestal
124 cm. 49 in. high

The mould for this was taken from an original at Holker Hall, Cumbria, and although this copy is probably less than twenty years old, the patina of lichen and moss makes it appear very much older.

One of a pair of carved stone urns
mid 19th century

Since these are oval they are perhaps intended more as planters than urns. The stylized lobed decoration alternating with more naturalistic flower heads would suggest a date early in Victoria's reign. The acanthus carved protruding corners on the base show the quality of execution and design.

One of a pair of composition stone urns
91 cm. 36 in. high

Unusual in design, with an everted body moulded with stylized leaves, this design works well and is weathered to just the right degree.

Istrian stone jardinière 19th-century
63 cm. 25 in. high

Produced for an export market around the turn of the century. This piece, carved in relief with armorials and scrolling foliage, is a pastiche of earlier styles.

Composition stone jardinière
79 cm. 31 in. high

The idea of a Victorian font has been adapted to an urn, the sides moulded with quatrefoils, which gives this piece a slightly ecclesiastical feel.

Terracotta model of the Townley Vase on pedestal
108 cm. 71 in. high

This is typical of the terracotta being produced in Italy in the early years of this century, and still being produced today. The Townley Vase is a well-known model after the Antique now in the British Museum. The pedestal was produced later in the same style.

Stoneware urn stamped 'Garnkirk'
91 cm. 36 in. high

An example of this urn was shown by Messrs. Ferguson, Miller and Co. in the 1851 Great Exhibition. In 1862 the company's moulds were obtained by the Garnkirk Fire-clay company near Glasgow in Scotland. The body of the urn depicts a seated Queen Victoria holding an orb, surrounded by figures of various nationalities bearing gifts. It epitomises the idea of Britain as the centre of the civilized world.

Stoneware urn on pedestal
152 cm. 60 in. high

Even a cursory glance at this piece makes one wonder what went wrong. It was made towards the end of the last century in a number of pieces, which over the years have become muddled up and lost, resulting in a hotchpotch of various components.

Stoneware urn on pedestal
102 cm. 40 in. high

Of a fairly standard form, this is stamped 'Published by J.M. Blashfield, Stamford 1869'. James Marriott Blashfield was an important manufacturer, first operating in London and then moving to Stamford, Lincolnshire, in 1858. He published a number of catalogues illustrating a variety of garden ornaments and architectural fittings. His most important commission was the formal garden and gate piers at Castle Ashby, Northampton.

Liberty's earthenware jardinière on stand
116 cm. 45½ in. high

Stamped 'Designed and Manufactured by Liberty & Co.' this was probably designed by Archibald Knox whose distinctive designs for Liberty's in the early 20th century extended across a wide range of articles.

Coade stone pedestal
105 cm. 41 in. high, stamped 'Coade's Lithodipyhra, London'

Lithodipyhra means stone twice fired. This is one of the firm's early models – a set of four are recorded at West Wycombe in 1781 – and it features in the Coade catalogue dating from the late 1770s. In a later Coade publication, *A Descriptive Catalogue of Coade's Artificial Stone Manufactory*, 1784, it is described as an elegant candelabrum composed of three figures on a pedestal, priced at 12 guineas.

Terracotta urn
97 cm. 38 in. high

It is unfortunate that this bears no manufacturer's stamp or mark, since the design and modelling is of high quality and the size impressive. The spreading base would suggest that it was probably a gate pier finial.

One of a pair of mid-19th-century stoneware urns on pedestals
117 cm. 46 in. high
Each stamped 'J. Stiff & Sons, Lambeth'

Stiff & Sons were one of a number of 'artificial stone' manufacturers following in the Coade tradition. The clay body is of the same consistency and is a little yellower than Coade stone. This pair of urns is well modelled and crisp in detail, but the urn is too small in relation to the pedestal.

Stoneware urn
76 cm. 30 in. high

Stamped 'Pulhams Terracotta, Broxbourne', and produced in the mid-19th century, this is sometimes referred to as 'Pulhamite'. The material is more akin to a stoneware than a terracotta since the clay is fired to a higher temperature, making it less porous and susceptible to frost and damage. Many 19th-century manufacturers including Blashfield called their wares 'terracotta', though they were technically stoneware.

Pair of stoneware versions of the Albani Vase
after an Antique model, 64 cm. 25 in. high

Produced in the middle of the last century and unfortunately not stamped, these are very similar to the more well-known Warwick Vase, differing mainly in the interlooping handles, which one of them has unfortunately lost.

Glazed stoneware 'Rustic' urn on stand
96 cm. 38 in. high

An amusing attempt to combine the shape of the urn with natural forms. The truncated tree stump base has holes for planting.

Terracotta oil storage jar
90 cm. 35 in. high

Large numbers of these are still to be seen in Tuscany, Italy, where they were originally made to store the olive oil produced in the area. They are also to be found in many other olive producing European countries. Many have found their way to England, but they are susceptible to frost damage if left outside for long periods of time.

Furniture

Coalbrookdale water plant pattern cast iron seat
144 cm. 56½ in. wide

Most of the designers for Coalbrookdale are unrecorded, but it is known that Christopher Dresser was responsible for this pattern. It incorporates a foliate element, but with Dresser's characteristically geometric approach to design.

Coalbrookdale 'Serpent and grape pattern' cast iron seat
130 cm. 51 in. high

This pattern could be bought in a variety of widths or the end supports only could be purchased, allowing the owner to choose his own width.

Coalbrookdale oak and ivy pattern cast iron seat
155 cm. 61 in. wide

Amongst the more elaborate of the Coalbrookdale designs and incorporating an apron. The enclosed arms with their distinctive grotesque head terminals are very prone to trap water and encourage rust.

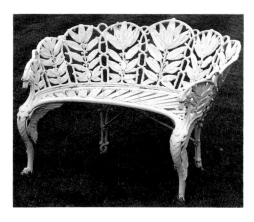

Coalbrookdale laurel pattern cast iron garden seat
118 cm. 46½ in. wide

A pleasing design combining naturalistic elements with grotesque arm terminals and wing cast cabriole legs. It could be purchased with a seat of wooden slats or scrolled pierced iron. The maker's stamps on this pattern are incorporated into the leaves on the back, and are easy to miss if the seat has a number of layers of paint.

Coalbrookdale fern and blackberry cast iron garden seat
150 cm. 59 in. wide (with chair en suite)

The most common of the Coalbrookdale seats of which large numbers have survived. None of this pattern is ever marked. Coalbrookdale had a very arbitrary policy about which patterns were stamped. This applies to urns, fountains and many other architectural fittings which they produced.

Coalbrookdale lily-of-the-valley pattern cast iron seat
c.1870

Coalbrookdale, the largest manufacturer of cast iron garden furniture, offered a number of garden seats and chairs, in a variety of sizes and finishes, with oak or pine seats and either painted or, in this case, originally with a 'bronzed' finish. Almost all the designs incorporated flowers and plants in their decoration, reflecting the growing awareness of the natural beauty of nature championed by John Ruskin and others. The method of production was, of course, entirely mechanized, but this did not stop such designs from selling in very large numbers.

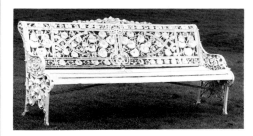

Coalbrookdale nasturtium pattern garden seat
180 cm. 71 in. wide

This pattern could be purchased in various sizes, but the centre of the back is always surmounted by a mask and stamped 'C.B. Dale' with a lozenge shaped registration stamp and registration number.

One of a pair of Coalbrookdale nasturtium pattern chairs

These examples have recently been shot-blasted and lacquered, which has brought out the quality of the casting; for instance the veins on the leaves, which are often obscured in painted examples. Also in evidence on the sides are the round-headed bronze nuts, often used by Coalbrookdale. Many of these benches are now being reproduced, as are a number of other patterns. Some are sold as reproduction whilst others are artificially aged, often by rusting with salt water, and then painted. Moulds taken from originals will faithfully reproduce the Coalbrookdale mask and registration stamps. Most fakes can be spotted by the lack of finish on the seams which makes them very sharp. They seldom use bronze nuts, and usually incorporate modern hexagonal machine made nuts.

Coalbrookdale Gothic pattern cast iron seat
157 cm. 62 in. wide

This pattern manages to combine the naturalistic foliate motifs common in most Coalbrookdale designs with Gothic style tracery, centred with a quasi-armorial shield.

Cast iron garden chair

Although the proportions are unusual and there is no foundry stamp, the quality of casting and detail is very good, and, despite the low back, the piece is extremely comfortable to sit on—an important consideration often overlooked in evaluating seat furniture.

Victorian cast iron seat
178 cm. 70 in.

A sophisticated design, incorporating panels of a sower, hoer and harvesters within a stylized foliate design. The rarity of this design suggests that it may have been specifically produced as an exhibition piece to illustrate the foundry's capabilities.

Lion Foundry cast iron garden seat
105 cm. 41½ in wide

Stamped 'Lion Foundry, Northampton, registered by W. Roberts'. The Lion Foundry was established in the early 1830s. The owner, John Brettel, went into partnership with William Roberts in 1849 and three years later Roberts took over the company. The roundels in the back of the seat represent Spring and Summer, and other examples are known incorporating the other seasons.

Cast iron garden seat
190 cm.75 in. wide

This seems French in inspiration, but some examples of this pattern bear English registration stamps. Although very intricate, incorporating a number of different motifs, the design works well.

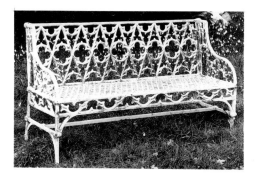

Cast iron garden bench
142 cm. 56 in. wide

Produced in large quantities in a variety of sizes and with chairs en suite, this pattern occasionally has a retailer's label but never a founder's mark. Its design follows the best traditions of Victorian Gothic, incorporating quatrefoils and tracery in the back in a way commonly associated with Pugin's decoration of the Houses of Parliament. It would have taken a few years for this high style of architecture to have percolated into garden design.

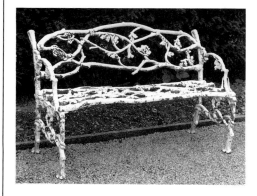

Cast iron seat
127 cm. 50 in. wide

Another popular 19th-century pattern entirely made up of truncated branches hand finished with metal collars. Unlike hand-wrought pieces, cast iron, becomes very brittle especially when old. The lack of any strong supporting members on the back or seat makes this design liable to damage very easily. The design repeated in the seat is also not conducive to comfort.

Reeded wrought iron seat
110 cm. 43½ in. wide

Dating from early in the 19th century and wrought by hand rather than being mass-produced like the later cast iron examples. Many of these seats conform to a very similar design and construction, but unlike the great furniture directories of Chippendale and Sheraton, no books or engravings exist to show how the pattern became disseminated all over the country. Most have a segmented back, plain slatted seat, and paw feet supported by a bowed stretcher. The design has a basic flaw on examples with a reeded slatted seat, since water gathers between the ridges of the iron, generating rust.

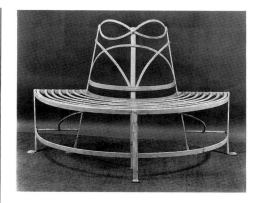

Reeded wrought iron seat
140 cm. 55 in. wide

A typical early 19th-century example, one of a pair originally intended to sit around the base of a tree.

One of a set of six wrought iron chairs

Very stylish in design and made early this century. They do however incorporate an interwoven strapwork seat associated with earlier designs.

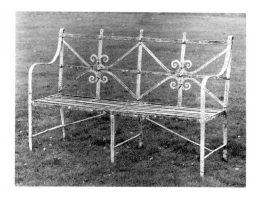

Reeded wrought iron garden seat, early 19th century
154 cm. 60½ in. wide

The simplicity of design is a pleasure to the eye. Most examples have overscroll terminals on the back and paw feet, but this one, instead of the usual segmented back, incorporates scrolling motifs. The paint finish, where earlier colours used are showing through, makes this a very desirable example.

One of a pair of sprung metal chairs

Originally produced by such firms as Bernard, Bishop & Barrards of Norwich. In 1878 this chair, finished in japanned green, retailed at 18 shillings. The sprung back and seat is comfortable to sit on when in good condition but the individual slats are liable to rust and can easily break.

Wrought iron garden seat
120 cm. 47 in. wide

A hotch-potch of parts, doubtless produced by a local blacksmith; the uprights and supports have been given a barley twist application of wirework which does nothing to enhance the appearance of the seat.

Carved Portland stone seat
183 cm. 72 in. wide

The reclining cherubs resemble those popular in the 17th century, but their very distinctive 19th-century faces reveal their true date. The design of the back and seat, with the scroll terminals sweeping from the

middle of the back down to the ends of the arms, is very liquid and successful, but the overall image is spoilt by the squat supports.

Carved stone bench
180 cm. 71 in. wide

The curved top is 18th-century Portland stone, carved along the edge with drapery swags, while the griffin supports are sandstone and date from the last century. Despite being a 'marriage' the two components work well together.

Portland stone seat
236 cm. 93 in. wide

A classic example of a Portland stone seat produced at the turn of the 18th/19th century, restrained in design with a plain panelled back and bead-and-reel and rope-twist borders on the seat edge. The capacity of Portland stone to withstand extreme climatic conditions without crumbling, and yet retain a weathered patination, is well illustrated in this example.

Composition stone seat
157 cm. 62 in. wide

Produced in Italy in the 20th century in moulds using an aggregate including marble chips and dust and in an eclectic mixture of styles from Renaissance to Egyptian revival. In its relatively short life it has achieved a patination of weathering which makes it considerably more acceptable than a starkly uniform brand new example.

Composition stone bench
356 cm. 140 in. wide

The middle of the centre section bears an impressed signature 'Descomps'. Joseph Descomps was working in France at the turn of the last century. This substantial piece is unusual in being cast (in three sections), rather than carved. The original would have been carved and moulds taken from it with which to make copies. Mould-making is an expensive process and a number of copies are usually produced to make it viable. Paradoxically, however, this piece is extremely rare, and this is the only example known.

Carved stone seat
142 cm. 56 in. wide

Late 18th/early 19th century in date, with a plain panelled back, the design is largely dependent on the magnificently noble winged lion end supports.

White marble seat
121 cm. 47½ in wide

Of Indian origin. Such seats differ little in style from the 17th to 19th century. Typical elements include the stylized animals, ogee finials and the back pierced in a trellis design.

Carved stone seat
340 cm. 134 in. wide

A magnificent example of an 18th-century carved seat, carved in sections and then put together with mortar. This example has been wrongly assembled since the line of blocks beneath the cresting should be at seat level beneath the panelled back.

Stone bench
114 cm. 55 in. wide

Carved in soft limestone from the Vicenza region of Italy, the detail is considerably crisper than on composition stone examples, and the softness of the stone allows it to weather relatively quickly.

White marble bench, late 19th century
165 cm. 65 in. wide

The borders of the rectangular top have been carved in relief with foliage, while the standard volute supports have been enhanced with scrolling acanthus.

Rosso Verona marble bench
140 cm. 55 in. wide

Produced in Italy late in the last century. The lions are Romanesque in style. Rosso Verona is a pinkish marble which becomes redder when wet.

Italian white marble chair
c. 1870

Reminiscent of a Renaissance throne, this eclectic mixture of styles proclaims power and opulence and elevates the concept of an ordinary 'common or garden' chair into something infinitely more grand. The back is surmounted by an armorial cartouche still waiting to be monogrammed. It would have had enormous appeal to the new class of industrial rich in the latter half of the last century.

Bronze and composition marble seat
152 cm. 60 in. high

Sculpted by Nicholas Dimbleby and exhibited at the 1981 Royal Academy Summer Exhibition, London. The back and base are moulded in a resin using marble dust, whilst the girl's legs, on which one sits, are cast in bronze. Although not very comfortable, the idea of combining a figurative sculpture with a practical function is a worthwhile one.

Suite of rustic tin glazed earthenware furniture

Most of these were manufacturered in Scotland by fairly obscure potteries and clayworks in the 1870s onwards, taking the 'rustic' concept to an extreme. They are very impractical because of their enormous weight.

Wooden garden seat
238 cm. 94 in.

Produced very much in the Lutyens style, early this century. The design goes back to the 17th century. There is srong evidence to suggest that Lutyens himself copied models of this period, such as those originally at Chiswick House, London, and visible in engravings of the time.

Coalbrookdale cast iron flower stand
102 cm. 40 in. wide

This rare example in circular form was made to stand in the centre of a conservatory or terrace. It is included in the 1875 Coalbrookdale catalogue.

Cast iron pub table
71 cm. 28 in. diameter

An interesting variation on the more
common 'Britannia' pattern, this design
incorporates the bearded head of W.G.
Grace, one of the most famous cricketers of
the last century. Probably tables like this
were ordered specifically for use at cricket
grounds over the country.

Victorian cast iron pub table
70 cm. 28 in. diameter

The most common design of pub table,
incorporating the figure of Britannia
supporting a shield emblazoned with the
Union Jack of Great Britain. The circular
tops were made in either wood or marble.
This example has the maker's plaque on the
under tier stamped Gaskell and Chambers
Ltd., Bar Fitters, Manchester. Although
made originally purely as public house
furniture, many have found their way into
gardens.

Coalbrookdale cast iron flower stand

The 1875 Coalbrookdale catalogue shows
that this figure originally supported a
latticework basket on his head, which at
some stage has been broken and removed. It
is worth noting that the triform base is also
used in some of the Coalbrookdale fountain
designs.

Cast iron plant stand, 19th century
101 cm. 40 in. high

Although copiously illustrated in foundry
catalogues of the last century, very few of
this sort of stand have survived. They were
designed either for a conservatory or to stand
against the wall of a house. Intricate in
design and with a lot of attention paid to
detail, this is a very good exmple of a rare
piece.

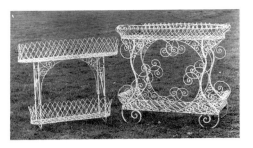

Two wirework plant stands
81 cm. 32 in. and 91 cm. 36 in. high

Flimsy in construction, these were produced
throughout the last century from a simple
Regency style to more elaborate Victorian
examples. Recent high prices for such pieces
have generated a number of reproductions in
which the wire is properly galvanised,
making them less susceptible to rust.

Wrought iron flowerbed surround
275 cm. 108 in. diameter

Photographed at Horsted Place near
Uckfield, East Sussex, this set of unusual
surrounds was designed by Carl Toms and
inspired by drawings in Humphry Repton's
Red Book for Brighton Pavilion. They were
made originally for the garden that Sir
Geoffrey Jellicoe designed for Lord and Lady
Rupert Nevill at Uckfield House and
subsequently moved to Horsted, where they
were again sited by Sir Geoffrey Jellicoe.

Selection of earthenware edging tiles
Each approximately 23 cm. 9 in. wide

Produced in very large quantities in the last
century in plain and saltglazed earthenware,
edging tiles have recently become very
popular, since they can give a new garden an
aura of age. The terracotta buff coloured
examples are more sought after than the
more industrial looking dark blue tiles.

Georgian lead cistern
123 cm. 48 in. wide

Cisterns were popular in large houses from the middle of the 17th century through to early in the 19th century. They were used to collect the rainwater from the roof, which was then used for domestic purposes in the house and garden. Many are dated. Most of the 18th-century examples have panelled fronts, sometimes incorporating the armorial crestings of the house for which they were made. This one probably comes from a military barracks, since it is decorated with cannon. The lead pipe now bent downwards on the left channelled the water in, a bronze tap in the centre enabled the water to be drawn off. Some examples are still in use in courtyards of houses, but many are simply filled with earth and planted out.

Bronze cannon, barrel
length 124 cm. 49 in.

Large quantities of disused cannon, either field pieces or removed from men-of-war, have found their way into gardens. Most, especially ship's cannon, have acquired new carriages. The bronze examples are obviously more desirable, especially if, as in this case, they have acquired a beautiful green patination. The breech bears the inscription 'Mountjoy Earl of Newport, Mr. Generall of the Ordnance John Browne made this piece 1642'.

Japanese 'kasuge' or lantern
108 cm. 72 in. high

Nearly always in granite, these mostly seem to conform to the same style and construction, coming apart in a number of sections. The smaller squatter variety are known as storm lanterns.

One of a pair of cast iron pedestals
98 cm. 38 in. high

Produced c. 1860, most probably by the Val d'Osne or Durenne foundries in France, they reflect the Egyptian taste of the day. They would originally have supported a cast iron figure, sometimes holding a light.

Portland stone sundial
155 cm. 61 in. high

A good substantial 18th-century sundial of generous proportions, although the lobed lower section has lost its foot and sits uncomfortably on the stone base. The dial is of the same period as the base, but, like many 18th-century bronze plates which sit horizontally, it tends to collect water in the grooves of the engraving, which over the years oxidizes the metal, making the maker's name and finer details difficult to read.

Staddle stone
102 cm. 40 in. high

Virtually unchanged in design for hundreds of years, staddle stones were originally used to raise tithe barns and granaries off the ground to stop rats and vermin from getting in. Vast numbers carved in the local stone of the area now stand flanking drives or simply as garden ornaments.

Select List of Suppliers

(Telephone numbers in brackets)

United Kingdom

Statuary and other ornament

Architectural Heritage
Boddington
Cheltenham
Gloucestershire GL51 0TJ
(0242 680741)

Crowther of Syon Lodge
London Road
Isleworth
Middlesex TW7 5BH
(01 560 7978)

T. Crowther and Son
282 North End Road
London SW6
(01 385 1375)

Seago
16 Lower Richmond Road
London SW15
(01 785 7155)

David Sharp Studios
30 Church Street
Lenton
Nottingham NG7 1SJ
(0602 470444)

J. Warren
Cedar Lodge
Littlebourne
Canterbury
Kent
(0227 721510)

Occasional sales of garden furniture and ornament

Christie's South Kensington
85 Old Brompton Road
London SW7 3LD
(01 581 7611)

Sotheby's
Summers Place
Billinghurst
West Sussex RH14 9AD
(040381 3933)

Stone ornament and buildings

Chilstone
Sprivers Estate
Horsmonden
Kent TN12 8DR
(089 272 3553)

Haddonstone Ltd.
The Forge House
East Haddon
Northampton NN6 8DB
(0604 770711)

Statuary and urns

Cranborne Manor
Cranborne
Wimborne
Dorset
(07254 248)

Sculpture

Simon Verity
The Old Schoolhouse
Rodbourne
Wiltshire
(06662 3837)

Gazebos

Ollerton
Samlesbury Bottoms
Preston
Lancashire PR5 0RN
(025485 2127/4121)

Conservatories and furniture

Machin Designs
Ransome's Dock
Parkgate Road
London SW11
(01 223 4340)

Bridges

Tiger Developments Ltd.
Deanland Road
Hailsham
East Sussex
(0285 872 555)

Treillage and trellis-work

Stuart Garden Architecture
Barrington Court
Barrington
Ilminster
Somerset TA19 0NQ
(0460 42003)

Seats and other furniture

Barnsley House Garden Furniture
Barnsley House
Cirencester
Gloucestershire
(0285 74561)

Chatsworth Carpenters
Estate Office
Edensor
Bakewell
Derbyshire
(024688 2242)

Makepeace Furniture Workshops
Parnham House
Beaminster
Dorset
(0308 862204)

United States

General ornament

Kenneth Lynch and Sons Inc.
PO Box 488
Wilton
Connecticut 06897-0488
(203 7628363)

Smith and Hawken
25 Corte Madera
Mill Valley
California 94941
(415 383 4415)

Terracotta, stone and other ornament

International Terra Cotta Inc.
690 North Robertson Boulevard
Los Angeles
California 90069-5088
(213 6573752)

Gazebos

Dalton Gazebos
7260-68 Oakley Street
Philadelphia
PA 19111
(215 3429804)

Wooden furniture

Chattahoochee Makers Company
1098 Huff Road NW
Atlanta
Georgia 30318
(404 3517016)

Iron ornament and furniture

Cassidy Brothers Forge Inc.
US Route 1
Rowley Massachusetts 01969-1796
(617 9487611)

Bibliography

Acton, Harold. *The Villas of Tuscany*. Thames and Hudson, London, 1973.

Adams, W.H. *The French Garden*. Scolar Press, London, 1979.

Alberti, L.B. *Dell' Architettura*. Venice, 1565.

Aslet, Clive. *Quinlan Terry*. Viking, London, 1986.

Berrall, Julia S. *The Garden*. Thames and Hudson, London, 1966.

Blomfield, Reginald. *The Formal Garden in England*. Macmillan, London, 1892.

Brookes, John. *Gardens of Paradise*. Weidenfeld and Nicolson, London, 1987.

Brown, Jane. *Gardens of a Golden Afternoon*. Allen Lane, London, 1982.

Casa Valdes, Marquesa de. *Spanish Gardens*. Antique Collectors Club, Woodbridge, 1987.

Chambers, Sir William. *Designs of Chinese Buildings*, London. 1757.

Chambers, Sir William. *Dissertation on Oriental Gardening*, London, 1772.

Crowe, Sylvia. *Garden Design*. Country Life, London, 1958.

Dami, Luigi. *The Italian Garden*. Bestetti and Tumminelli, Milan, 1925.

Downing, A.J. *A Treatise on the Theory and Practice of Landscape Gardening Adapted to North America*. New York, 1841.

Fouquier, M. and Duchêne, A. *Des Divers Styles de Jardins*. Paris, 1914.

Girard, Jacques. *Versailles Gardens: Sculpture and Mythology*. Sotheby's, London, 1985.

Goethein, Marie Luise. *A History of Garden Art*. (2 vols). J.M. Dent, London, 1928.

Hadfield, Miles. *Gardening in Britain*. Hutchinson, London, 1960.

Hunt, John Dixon. *Garden and Grove*. J.M. Dent, London, 1986.

Hunt, Peter (ed.). *The Book of Garden Ornament*. J.M. Dent, London, 1974.

Hussey, Christopher. *English Gardens and Landscapes, 1700-1750*. Country Life, London, 1967.

Hyams, Edward. *The English Garden*. Thames and Hudson, London, 1964.

Jashemski, Wilhelmina F. *The Gardens of Pompeii*. Caratzas Bros, New York, 1979.

Jekyll, Gertrude. *Garden Ornament*. Country Life, London, 1918. (Reprinted 1982)

Jellicoe, Geoffrey and Susan. *The Landscape of Man*. Thames and Hudson, London, 1975.

Jellicoe, Geoffrey and Susan, Goode, P., and Lancaster, M. (eds). *The Oxford Companion to Gardens*. Oxford, 1986.

Jones, Barbara. *Follies and Grottoes*. Constable, London, 1979.

Jourdain, Margaret. *The Work of William Kent*. Country Life, London, 1948.

Langley, Batty. *New Principles of Gardening*. London, 1728.

Langley, Batty. *Gothic Architecture*, London, 1742.

Lehrman, Jonas. *Earthly Paradise*. Thames and Hudson, London, 1980.

Loudon, J.C. *The Suburban Gardener and Villa Companion*. 1838.

Masson, Georgina. *Italian Gardens*. Thames and Hudson, London, 1961.

Mawson, Thomas H. *The Art and Craft of Garden Making*. Batsford, London, 1901.

Mollet, André. *Le Jardin de plaisir*, Paris, 1651.

Page, Russell. *The Education of a Gardener*. Collins, London, 1983.

Papworth, John. *Hints on Ornamental Gardening*, London, 1823.

Pereire, Anita. *Private Gardens of France*. Weidenfeld and Nicolson, London, 1983.

Pliny the Younger. *Letters*. Trans. Penguin, Harmondsworth, 1963.

Pope, Alexander. *Essay on Criticism*, London, 1711.

Pope, Alexander. *Epistle to Burlington*, London, 1732.

Prest, John. *The Garden of Eden*. Yale, 1981.

Price, Uvedale. *Essays on the Picturesque*. London, 1794.

Shenstone, William. *Unconnected Thoughts on Gardening*, London, 1764.

Shepherd, J.C. and Jellicoe, G.A. *Italian Gardens of the Renaissance*. Academy Editions, London, 1986.

Sitwell, Sir George. *On the Making of Gardens*. John Murray, London, 1909.

Stroud, Dorothy. *Capability Brown*. Country Life, London, 1957.

Stroud, Dorothy. *Humphry Repton*. Country Life, London, 1962.

Switzer, Stephen. *Ichnographia Rustica*, London, 1718.

Temple, Sir William. *Upon The Gardens of Epicurus*, London, 1692.

Triggs, H. Inigo. *The Formal Garden in England and Scotland*. Batsford, London, 1902. (Facsimile, 1988)

Triggs, H. Inigo. *The Art of Garden Design in Italy*. Longmans, London, 1906.

Triggs, H. Inigo. *Garden Craft in Europe*. Batsford, London, 1913.

Tunnard, Christopher. *Gardens in the Modern Landscape*. Architectural Press, London, 1938.

Walpole, Horace. *On Modern Gardening*, London, 1771.

Wharton, Edith. *Italian Villas and Their Gardens*. New York, 1904.

Wilson, Michael I. *William Kent*. Routledge and Keegan Paul, London, 1984.

Woodbridge, Kenneth. *Princely Gardens*. Thames and Hudson, London, 1986.

A note on photographic sources

The photographs in the last section, pp. 218-251, were supplied by Sotheby's. Illustrations from books are identified in the captions. All the rest, in colour and black-and-white, are by Hugh Palmer, with the following exceptions:

Alinari 98 (bottom); Bundesbiltstelle, Bonn 36 (left); Peter Clayton 62 (left); *Country Life* 35 (upper right); Edward Diestelkamp 49 (top), 70 (left), 108 (top right), 117 (bottom right); Gundermann Verlag 118; Hansa Luftbild 19 (top); Peter Hayden 36 (right), 77, 99, 100 (top), 120 (top left), 150, 157 (bottom left); A.F. Kersting 22 (left); Georgina Masson 28, 29 (top), 90, 91, 98 (top), 130; Metropolitan Museum of Art, New York 26; George Plumptre 139 (left); Dr E. Richter 29 (bottom); Helga Schmidt-Glassner 33; Edwin Smith 34 (both), 37, 63, 87 (right), 94, 95; Inigo Triggs 35 (bottom); Jeremy Whitaker 47.

The authors and photographer would like to thank the many garden owners whose co-operation and kindness made the year's work so enjoyable.

Index

Page numbers in *italic* indicate illustrations